T0119656

# Symbol & Archetype

# Symbol & Archetype

## A STUDY OF THE MEANING
## OF EXISTENCE

---

### MARTIN LINGS

FONS VITAE

First published in 2005 by
Fons Vitae
49 Mockingbird Valley Drive
Louisville, KY 40207
http://www.fonsvitae.com

Copyright Fons Vitae 2006

Library of Congress Control Number: 2005937564

ISBN 1-887752-79-X

For the cover image, refer to chapter twelve.

With thanks, for the preparation of this new volume,
to Justin Majzub and Elena Lloyd-Sidle.

This book was typeset by Neville Blakemore, Jr.

Printed in Canada.

# Contents

# *Preface*

The answer to the question 'What is Symbolism?', if deeply understood, has been known to change altogether a man's life; and it could indeed be said that most of the problems of the modern world result from ignorance of that answer. As to the past however, there is no traditional doctrine which does not teach that this world is the world of symbols, inasmuch as it contains nothing which is not a symbol. A man should therefore understand at least what that means, not only because he has to live in the herebelow but also and above all because without such understanding he would fail to understand himself, he being the supreme and central symbol in the terrestrial state.

Needless to say, this little book does not claim to be exhaustive. Its purpose is to enable the reader to dwell on certain basic aspects of symbolism in relation to the Divinity, the hierarchy of the universe, the function of man, his faculties and his qualities, the conditions to which he is subject, the natural objects which surround him, his works of art, and his final ends, all with reference to the great living religions of the world, and in particular to Christianity and Islam.

The first chapter will serve as an introduction. We will simply preface it with a statement which would once have been a platitude, but which now, to say the least, needs no apology: symbolism is the most important thing in existence; and it is at the same time the sole explanation of existence.

## CHAPTER ONE

# *What is Symbolism?*

*The seven Heavens and the earth and all that is therein glorify Him, nor is there anything but glorifieth Him with praise; yet ye understand not their glorification.*
(Qur'ān: XVII, 44)

The above verse is an answer to the question asked by our chapter-heading; it also justifies to a certain extent, in its last sentence, the writing of the chapter, for a thing's glorification of God—which *ye understand not*—is precisely its symbolism. This may be deduced from the Islamic 'holy utterance', so called because in it the Divinity speaks on the tongue of the Prophet: *I was a Hidden Treasure and I loved to be known, and so I created the world.*[1] Thus the universe and its contents were created in order to make known the Creator, and to make known the good is to praise it; the means of making it known is to reflect it or shadow it; and a symbol is the reflection or shadow of a higher reality.

The doctrine of symbolism may also be concluded from other verses in which the Qur'ān affirms that every single thing on earth has been sent down in finite measure from the Stores or Treasuries of the Infinite, sent down as a loan rather than a gift, for nothing herebelow can last, and everything must in the end revert to its Supreme Source. In other words, the Archetype is always the Heir who inherits back the symbol in which It manifested Itself: *Nor is there anything but with Us are the Treasuries thereof, and We send it not down save in known measure... and verily it is We who give life and make to die, and We are the Inheritor* (XV:21,23). We may likewise quote the following Quranic definition of the Divinity: *He is the First and the Last and the Outwardly Manifest and the Inwardly Hidden* (LVII:3). The first, second and fourth of these Names are related to the Hidden Treasure. As to *the Outwardly Manifest*, the mystery of the Divine Presence in the world of symbols is partly explained in the words *God created not the heavens and the earth and what lieth between them save from Truth and an appointed term* (XXX:8). It can thus be said that the whole fabric of the universe is woven out of Eternity and ephemerality, Infinitude and finitude, Absoluty and relativity.

Man himself as he was created—True Man as the Taoists name him—is the greatest of earthly symbols. The universal doctrine that he was made *in the image of God* (Genesis 1:27) signifies this pre-eminence: man is the symbol of the sum of all the attributes, that is, of the Divine Nature in its Totality, the Essence, whereas the animate and inanimate creatures that surround him reflect only one aspect or certain aspects of that Nature. Taken all together these symbols constitute the greater outer world, the macrocosm, of which man, God's representative on earth, is the centre; and that centre is itself a little world, a microcosm, analogous in every respect to the macrocosm which is, like it, a total image of the Archetype.

It is through its centre that a world lies open to all that transcends it. For the macrocosm man is that opening; as to the microcosm, its centre is man's Heart—not the bodily organ of that name but his soul's central faculty[2] which, in virtue of its centrality, must be considered as being above and beyond the psychic domain. The openness of the Eye of the Heart, or the wake of the Heart as many traditions term it, is what distinguishes primordial man—and by extension the Saint—from fallen man. The significance of this inward opening may be understood from the relationship between the sun and the moon which symbolize respectively the Spirit and the Heart: just as the moon looks towards the sun and transmits something of its reflected radiance to the darkness of the night, so the Heart transmits the light of the Spirit to the night of the soul. The Spirit itself lies open to the Supreme Source of all light, thus making, for one whose Heart is awake, a continuity between the Divine Qualities and the soul, a ray which is passed from Them by the Spirit to the Heart, from which it is diffused in a multiple refraction throughout the various channels of the psychic substance. The virtues which are thereby imprinted on the soul are thus nothing other than projections of the Qualities, and inversely each of these projected images is blessed with intuition of its Divine Archetype. As to the mind, with its reason, imagination and memory, a measure of the 'moonlight' which it receives from the Heart is passed on to the senses and through them as far as the outward objects which they see and hear and feel; and at this furthest contact the ray is reversed, for the things of the macrocosm are recognised as symbols, that is, as kindred manifestations of the Hidden Treasure, each of which has its counterpart in the microcosm. Otherwise expressed, for primordial man everything, inward or outward, was transparent: in experiencing a symbol he experienced its Archetype. He was thus able to rejoice in being outwardly surrounded and inwardly adorned by Divine Presences.

The eating of the fruit of the forbidden tree was the attachment to a symbol for its own sake apart from its higher meaning. That violation of the norm barred man's access to his inward centre, and the consequent blurring of his vision made him no longer able to fulfil adequately his original function as mediator between Heaven and earth. But at the fall of the microcosm, the macrocosm remained unfallen; and though its symbols had become less transparent to man's perceiving, they retained in themselves their original perfection. Only primordial man does justice to that perfection; but at the same time he is independent of it, in virtue of being himself a symbol of the Divine Essence which is absolutely Independent of the Divine Qualities. Fallen man on the other hand has a lesson to learn from the great outer world which surrounds him, for its symbols offer him an enlightenment which will be of guidance to him on his path of return to what he has lost, inasmuch as their perfection can further the perfecting of their counterparts within him which have suffered from the Fall. The clouds of the macrocosm are never permanent; they come only to go, the luminaries still shine, and the directions of space have lost nothing of their measurelessness. But in fallen man the soul is no longer the vast image of the Infinite that it was created to be, and the inward firmament is veiled. That veiling is the decisive result of the Fall, which did not sever the connection between soul and Spirit, between human perception and the Archetypes, but placed there a barrier that is more or less opaque—increasingly opaque as far as the majority is concerned, this increase being the gradual degeneration which inevitably takes place throughout each cycle of time. But in the context of our theme the barrier can and must be described as more or less transparent, since it would be pointless to speak of symbolism where there cannot be at least some intuition, however faint, of the Archetypes. Moreover the science of symbols is inextricably linked with the path of return which, being against the cyclic current, makes for an increase of transparency.

If the symbols of the macrocosm, taken collectively or separately, are reminders for the spiritual traveler of man's lost perfection, it might none the less be said that the most direct reminders will be microcosmic, that is, True Man himself, personified by the Prophets, the Saints and, more immediately, by the living Spiritual Master. But although there is no doubt a wealth of truth in this, it would be a simplification to reduce macrocosmic symbols to a second place in any absolute sense as regards their spiritual significance for man, since much will depend on the individual and on circumstances. Moreover otherness, as well as sameness, has its own special impact. The Qur'ān affirms the efficacy of both; *We shall show them Our signs on the horizons and in themselves* (XLI:53).

Let us consider, to take a particular example, the virtue of dignity which might be described as majesty in repose, and which man, if he would be true to his nature, must seek to perfect in himself side by side with the other virtues which reflect the other Divine Qualities. The swan incarnates just a particular aspect of dignity, but it does so to perfection and by isolating that perfection, it makes for man a powerfully clear-cut impression that is all the more irresistible for being presented in a non-human mode, that is, in a mode which is beyond our reach. That very beyondness can lend it wings, in the eye of the observer, for return to its Archetype. The same may be said of all the other great earthly symbols that are not human, such as sky, plain, ocean, desert, mountain, forest, river and what they encompass, each an eloquent 'word' in this language that the members of the white, yellow and black races share in common.

Since nothing can exist except in virtue of its Divine root, does that mean that everything is a symbol? The answer is yes and no—yes for the reason just given, and no because 'symbol' means 'sign' or 'token', which implies an operative power to call something to mind, namely its Archetype. In the light of the initially quoted verse *Nor is there anything but glorifieth Him with praise*, we could say that whether its 'praise' is powerful or faint. The word symbol is normally reserved for that which is particularly impressive in its 'glorification'.

The distinction we have just made can be more clearly understood with reference to the spider's web as an image of the created universe[3], an image that is all the more apt inasmuch as the web is woven out of the substance of its 'creator'. The concentric circles represent the hierarchy of the different worlds, that is, the different planes of existence; the more outward the circle, the lower its hierarchic degree, each circumference being in itself a disconnected outward (therefore 'downward') projection of the centre. The radii of the web on the other hand are images of the radiance of the Divine Mercy, and they portray the relationship of connection between the centre and all that exists. But it is significant that even if, on the basis of the web, a symbolic figure be drawn with the number of radii increased to the limit of what it is possible to set down on paper, there will still be, between the radii, gaps which increase in due proportion to the remoteness of the world in question from the 'Hidden Treasure' which it was created to reveal. In the world of matter, which marks the lowest limit of the downward and outward radiation of the Divine Principle, there will therefore be wider 'gaps' than anywhere else. Needless to say, there are in fact no voids, so that to justify our image it must be added that each radius has its own aura and that the intervening space between two radii is thus filled by the two presences in question. But not to be situated on the radius itself means necessarily not to be an outstandingly direct reflection of the transcendent Archetype; and the qualitative disparities between the various things of this world can be partly explained in the light of this image.

Since we are concerned with what is symbolic and what is not, it should be understood that we are not considering here disparities such as those between the animal, vegetable and mineral kingdoms or between different sections of the same kingdom—mammals, birds and insects, for example. The lion, the eagle and the bee are all true symbols, each being a summit in its own domain which means, in the language of our figure,[4] that it lies on one of the radii, whence its power to place us on the same ray of the creative Spirit so that our aspirations may thereby ascend inversely back to the source. But not everything is capable of offering us this possibility; and the disparities we have been speaking of lie between true symbols and kindred beings which are considerably less well favoured.[5] It is in the nature of things that some of the contents of the world that is furthest from the Principle should bear signs of that remoteness.

By way of summing up, still with reference to the concentric circles and the radii of the web, it could be said that all created things are both disconnected projections of their creative Principle while being at the same time Its connected radiations. On this basis the symbol could be defined as that in which the relationship of connection predominates over that of disconnection, whereas the predominance of disconnectedness precludes, as it were by definition, any outstanding power to connect us with the Archetype, and it is that power which may be said to confer, on its possessor, the status of symbol.

To see that symbolism is inseparable from religion we have only to remember that the word religion indicates the *re*-establishment of a ligament with the Supreme Arche-type, and one has to resort to a symbol for that purpose. Primordial man, in virtue of being directly aware of his own connectedness, was the personification of the link which religion aims at restoring, whence his capacity to act as mediator between the Divinity and Its microcosmic and macrocosmic reflections which are, respectively, man (or the soul) and the earthly state in its entirety including its human centre.

If religion means spirituality, then primordial man was the embodiment of religion. But if this word be under-stood strictly in its etymological sense he cannot be said to have had any religion, for there is clearly no need to re-establish a connection which has never been impaired. Nor did he need in any negative sense of that word, a science of symbols; but in virtue of his being a total image of the Divine, he could not fail to reflect the Hidden Treasure's joy—*I loved to be known*—at perceiving Itself mirrored in created things. Otherwise expressed, beneath the Supreme Beatitude of Gnosis, that is, the consciousness of identity with the Absolute Infinite One, his happiness as a soul in bliss coincided with symbolism, that of Paradise itself and of all that it contained including himself and other holy microcosms.

An essential aspect of every religion is the performance of rites. But if it be said that primordial man had no need of rites, it must be added that for him every act was poten-tially a rite in virtue of his awareness of its symbolic sig-nificance. The possession of a spiritual nature above his human nature enabled his consciousness to transcend the earthly state and with it the temporal condition. The do-main of the Spirit encompasses the whole of time and is therefore as it were simultaneously 'before' the creation of man and 'after' his resurrection.[6] Seen from that angle, symbols have 'already' been reabsorbed into their spiritual archetypes; but such a standpoint is beyond the reach of fallen man, except in theory, since he no longer has access to the Heart which is the gateway to the Spirit. In other words, the Saint is able to lend his wings to a symbol, and those wings, with which the primordial soul was naturally fledged, were lost at the Fall.

If the Saint does not, strictly speaking, need the prescribed rites of a religion, he can none the less rejoice in them, and he is their exemplary performer. But as to fallen man, inasmuch as they are Heaven's answer to his wingless predicament, he needs them imperatively above all things else. They could be defined as symbolic acts or enacted symbols, providentially endowed with wings for return to their Source, wings which the performer of the rite acquires by identifying himself with the act in question. Otherwise expressed, a rite is as a life-line thrown down from Heaven: it is for the worshipper to cling to the life-line; the rest is in the hands of the Thrower. Since a rite is always performed with a view to God, it amounts to a re-enactment of the connection between the symbol (in this case man) and the Supreme Archetype, a vibrating of that unsevered but dormant link, which needs the constant repetition of these vibrant acts to rouse it, once and for all, from sleep to wake.

In considering the relationship between rites and the categories of symbols already mentioned, it must be remembered that the Hidden Treasure may always radiate anew certain aspects of Itself in whatever degree of intensity is needed to overwhelm human limitations, and in whatever mode is best adapted to the particular receptivity of a given time and place. Such are the Divine interventions which establish the religions on earth, and without which no religion could take root. The altogether exceptional power with which Providence intervenes at these cyclic moments necessarily brings into being symbols for which the definitions already given will not suffice. It is true that every symbol has, as we have seen, a mysterious identity with its Archetype. But of symbols in general it can and must be said that they are merely symbols and not the Archetype. Being 'of this world' they are subject to all its conditions and limitations. A Revelation also—together with the sacramental symbols with which it operates— being in this world, though not 'of it', is bound to take on a finite form. It is none the less a 'stranger' herebelow, for the whole point of its earthly existence is that it should amount to an other-worldly intrusion, that it should be a real presence of the Infinite in the finite, of the Transformal in the formal. Moreover what is true of Revelation, such as the Vedas, the Pentateuch and the Psalms, the Tao-Te-King, the Qur'ān, is likewise true of the descents of the Divine Word in human form such as the Hindu Avatāras, including the Buddha, and by extension Jesus. Considering the part they are called upon to play in their various religions, it would indeed be pointless to say of any of these, within the context of the perspective in question, that they are 'merely symbols'. Therefore, in respect of our having said that a symbol worthy of the name is that in which the Archetype's radiation predominates over the projection, it is necessary to add that the sacramental symbol proceeds from its Source, relatively speaking, by pure radiation. To express this distinction the words 'begotten not made' can be transposed from the Christian creed and applied universally, for such symbols may well be said to be 'of one substance' with the Archetype.

With regard to the Eucharist as an example of a sacramental symbol, it is worthy of note that the otherworldliness of its bread and wine is affirmed not only in Christianity but also, and even more absolutely, by the Islamic Revelation, which mentions the Last Supper—in a chapter that is named after it, 'The Banquet'—as the immediate result of the following prayer of Jesus at the request of his disciples: *O God, our Lord, send down to us a banquet from Heaven which will be a feast for the first of us and the last of us,[7] and a sign from Thee* (V:114). Also highly significant, as regards Revelation in general, is the Islamic dogma that the Qur'ān is 'not created'. The same identity of the sacramental symbol with its Archetype constitutes the basis of the universal esoteric rite of invoking the Divine Name. Hindu *japa-yoga* (union by invocation) and its equivalents in all other esoterisms have, as their guarantee of efficacy, the truth which Sufism expresses with the words 'the Name is the Named'.

## CHAPTER TWO

# *The Decisive Boundary*

The different degrees in the hierarchy of universal existence could be subdivided again and again. But what matters doctrinally is to be aware of the main divisions, starting from the Absolute Itself which is beyond existence and
beyond Being, and which alone is Real, in the full sense of
the word. This is the degree of the Transpersonal Self, which
transcends all relativity. Below It, but still in the domain of
Divinity, is the relative Absolute[1], that is, the Personal God,
the Creator from Whom proceeds all createdness, all existence.[2] Creation marks the division between the Divine
and the existent, between Worshipped and worshipper. The
subsequent great division in the hierarchy is the polariza-
tion of all existence into Heaven and earth, or Spirit and
soul—from our point of view this world and the next,
though the last word may be taken in a wider sense to include all that transcends this world, both created and
Uncreated. Finally there is the division between soul and
body, between the psychic world and the material world.

Each world in the hierarchy of the universe is a reflection of the one above it, and each of its contents reflects, in
the higher world, a counterpart which is the immediate
source of its existence but which, in its turn, is no more
than the reflection of a yet more real counterpart from a
yet higher plane of existence. There is thus, for each symbol in the world of matter, a whole series of archetypes
one above the other, like the rungs of a ladder, leading up

to the Supreme Archetype in the Divine Essence. With regard to the term archetype however, we are obliged to make an important reservation, the reason for which can clearly be seen in the light of the significance of the *Symplegades*, the Clashing Rocks of Greek mythology. In his masterly article on these rocks[3], Ananda Coomaraswamy shows that they have their equivalents in many other ancient traditions where the symbol takes also the form of clashing mountains, clashing icebergs, clashing waters, clashing portals and, in the temporal domain, the clashing together of day and night between which the two twilights offer narrow gates of passage. What is above all significant in our present context is the extreme difficulty and danger of the passage. It is virtually impossible to reach what lies beyond the rocks without the help of Heaven; and aspiration towards that beyond—so Coomaraswamy's article shows us—was a dominant factor in the lives of all the peoples of antiquity—we might say of all peoples except those who are typical of the modern civilization. The rocks are clearly the equivalent of the *strait gate* (Matt. VII:13-14) of the Gospel; and like that gate they are situated precisely between the soul and the Spirit, where this world ends and the next world begins. To tell of the rocks is thus to affirm that the place where they operate is what might be called a particularly crucial rung in the ladder of existence. From the human point of view, that is indeed the decisive boundary; nothing of lasting value exists or can be achieved this side of the Symplegades, while beyond them there is no evil, no suffering and no death. It was the Fall which galvanized these rocks into activity, and they are in fact the equivalent of what barred the return of fallen man to Eden—in the words of Genesis;—*Cherubims and a flaming sword which turned every way to keep the way of the tree of life* (III:24). The Tree and the Fountain mark the centre of the earthly state; but a centre, since it is the point of access to higher realities, is always above the rest of its domain. Thus on the one hand Eden is the Terrestrial Paradise, while on the other hand it is spoken of as if it belonged to the next world, for like its central Tree and Fountain it is beyond the flaming sword and the clashing rocks. So, analogously, is the Heart, the centre of the soul; but the soul as such, together with its body, is on this side of the barrier. It ranks above the body, which is its shadow or reflection; but it shares with the body the limitation of being natural and not in any sense supernatural.

It follows by way of consequence that although every material symbol reflects its counterparts in the soul—and it may reflect more than one at different levels of the psychic domain—such counterparts are not normally referred to as archetypes. This term is strictly reserved, in traditional practice, for what lies beyond the crucial barrier that is represented by the rocks which Athene held apart for the Argonauts to pass, by *the strait gate* of which it is said *few are they that find it*, and by the waters of the Red Sea[4] which opened for the children of Israel on their way to the Promised Land but which closed upon Pharaoh and his host who had no warrant to pass.

There is more than one imperative practical reason—and for practical we might say methodic—why such words as archetype should not be squandered on the psychic domain. The prefix 'arch' signifies both exaltation and primacy, which confers on it also a sense of finality from the mystical standpoint of looking towards our first origins with a view to reintegration, whereas the soul is, from the same standpoint, that which has to be surpassed. There can be no advancing upon the spiritual path unless all one's aspirations and energies be concentrated on what lies beyond the ego. But there is something in the soul which shrinks,

14

not unnaturally, from the ordeal of the dread passage, and which will snatch at any pretext for putting off 'the evil day', and for enticing the spiritual traveler into its own seemingly endless labyrinthine recesses. Moreover the microcosm's fear of surpassing itself finds an ally in the unwillingness of the macrocosm, that is, all that lies on this side of the barrier, to allow any part of itself to escape from its hold. Nor, to say the least, is it for nothing that the Fall unleashed for mankind a downward and outward impetus which makes any approach to the decisive boundary a difficult upstream movement. The personifier of that impetus, whether he be called demi-urge or devil, will not fail to exploit the above-mentioned disinclinations as a means of obstructing the path of return to our origins.

The modern world presents another obstacle for him to exploit, one which did not previously exist, inasmuch as psychology—in all but name—was in the hands of spiritual men. In traditional civilizations it was the priest or his equivalent, and no one else, who was thought qualified to give advice about the soul, which was never considered independently of man's final ends, that is, without reference to the higher degrees of reality. The ego could not turn a blind eye to its own limitations because it was never allowed to forget its place in the hierarchy of existence. Moreover those responsible for 'the cure of souls' could take for granted a general knowledge of the doctrine of original sin. It was as if every patient had been told in advance, to use the language of our theme, 'you are on the wrong side of the boundary, and until you are able to reach the other side you will continue to be somewhat subhuman and must expect the consequences'. All advice was given on that basis of realism.

Modern psychology, on the contrary, dismisses the doctrine in question and with it the 'rocks'. The higher reaches of the universe are relegated to the realm of mere supposition, and the microcosm, soul and body, is isolated from all that transcends it. The soul is thus treated as the highest known thing. The average psychoanalyst may not deliberately set out to inflate it with self-importance but in fact his so-called science acts like a conspiracy in that direction. Another closely related illusion inculcated by it is that of being self-sufficient and normal. The soul is made unrealistically expectant of freedom from problems which are bound to beset it, and the absence of which would be discreditable.[5]

The point to be made here however, is that although modern psychology is eager to throw metaphysics to the winds, it is not prepared to impoverish its own vocabulary by abstention from high-sounding words of metaphysical import. Consequently 'archetype' and 'transcendent', to mention only two examples[6], are currently used in relation to things which, while being higher than others, none the less belong to the domain of nature which is by definition untranscendent and therefore not capable of being the repository of archetypes.[7]

## CHAPTER THREE

# The Symbolism of the Pairs

*Glory be to Him who hath created all the pairs, of that which the earth groweth, and of themselves, and of that whereof they know not.* (Qur'ān: XXXVI:36)

Creation means manifestation, by the Creator, of His own unmanifested attributes, as is clear from the already quoted Holy Tradition: *I was a Hidden Treasure and I loved to be known, and so I created the world.* But the title of this chapter may raise the question: 'What of the Divine Oneness? Should not this be dwelt on, before there is any consideration of duality?' The answer is that the symbolizing of the One is too obvious to need exposition at any length. On the one hand this Archetype is reflected in the unity which everything possesses in itself; on the other hand the One's exclusive aspect of One-and-Onliness imprints uniqueness on each single one of Its manifestations so that no two things can possibly be identical, however similar they may be. Nor can any of the dualities which are the theme of this chapter escape from the One, for the very notion of 'pair' implies complementarity, which is a condition and an anticipation of union.

The particular aspect of creation referred to in the opening Quranic verse may be said to have its roots in the Divine Name, Possessor of Majesty and Bounty (*Dhū l-Jalāli wa l-Ikrām*), which indicates a polarity of complements

17

mysteriously hidden in the Oneness of the Creator. On the basis of this polarity a distinction is made in Islamic doctrine between the Majestic Names and the Beautiful Names. Bounty and Beauty are closely related aspects of what the Taoists term Passive Perfection (*Khouen*), of which the complement is Active Perfection (*Khien*). The Hindu terms *Purusha* and *Prakriti* denote the same archetypal pair. They themselves are unmanifested, but it is from them that manifestation (creation) proceeds or, more precisely, it is born from the womb of *Prakriti* under the influence of *Purusha*. The great symbol of *Prakriti* is water.

The same symbolism but at a lower level, within the domain of creation, is used in Genesis. *The Spirit of God moved upon the face of the waters* (I:2) and from the subsequent division of the waters results the pair Heaven and earth, and their personal analogue Spirit and soul. A figure universally used to portray such 'vertical' polarity in which one term transcends the other is the Seal of Solomon. It expresses this relationship at every level, and in particular it frequently serves to denote the pair Creator-creation, or God-man. Its close-knit symmetrical beauty, which often figures in the decorative arts of many different traditions, goes hand in hand with its symbolic power, for it expresses not only direct analogy—man made in the image of God— but also inverse analogy by reason of which the First is reflected on earth above all by the last in order of creation, just as, on the plane of matter, the top of a mountain is seen at the bottom of a pool of water that reflects it. The Seal is also expressive of the mysterious interpenetration between the higher and lower poles of a vertical pair, and because of this it is used as a symbol of the two natures of Christ, Divine and human. But its significance is by no means limited to relationships at different levels, since the upturned apex of one triangle and the upturned base of the other, that is, the predominance of dynamic contraction in one and of static expansion in the other, make them respectively symbols of activity and passivity, or male and female. The Seal is thus a figure of the union of the Active and Passive Perfections, and of the Divine Name, Possessor of Majesty and Bounty.

Pre-eminent amongst the created pairs are the polarizations of the different persons of the Spirit, each one of which has inevitably both a masculine and a feminine aspect. According to Hinduism, *Buddhi* (Spirit, Intellect) is the summit and the synthesis of all manifestation, being the manifested offspring of *Purusha* and *Prakriti*. It corresponds to the Logos in its created aspect, and it has three persons, Brahmā, Vishnu and Shiva, each of which has its *Shaktī* (productive will), that is, its feminine consort. These are, respectively, Sarasvatī, Lakshmī and Parvati.[1] There is also an apotheosis of Sita and Radha, the earthly consorts of Rama and Krishna, the seventh and eighth *Avatāras* (descents) of Vishnu, who are thus frequently invoked by the two-fold names Sita-Ram and Radha-Krishna. We are reminded, despite the difference of human relationship, of the name Jesu-Maria.

The starting point of esoterism is the soul's consciousness of its need to regain the lost Paradise of Eden wherein it had access, through the Tree of Life and the Waters of Life, to the Spirit. In other words, the initial aspiration is a longing of the soul for the Spirit—'for God', we might say, for the Spirit opens onto the Divinity. If the seeker is a man, in order to enlist more easily all the powers of the soul for the spiritual path, the Spirit, considered in its complementary feminine aspect, may be personified by a woman. An example is to be found in Dante's *Divine Comedy*, where Beatrice, the beloved of Dante, symbolizes an aspect of the Spirit. From the Earthly Paradise, on the top of the Mountain of Purgatory, it is she who guides him through the Heavens.

Since no symbol can account for every aspect of its archetype, the Seal, for all its remarkable symbolic scope, can be instructively supplemented by another figure which may be obtained from it by turning the two triangles upside down so that their apexes meet in a point. The upturned lower triangle, like a pair of Christian hands in prayer, expresses the upward aspiration of the soul towards the Spirit, while in a parallel way it stands for the Mountain of Purgatory. The downturned upper triangle is an image of Mercy and Grace. As a whole, the figure is a diagram of the two seas—Heaven and earth or Spirit and soul—mentioned in the Qur'ān (XXV:53 & LV:19-20) as meeting but unable to overpass the barrier which prevents them from encroaching upon each other. Also powerfully figured, in the central point where the apexes meet, is the *strait gate* of the Gospels.

Despite the inequality of Spirit and soul, their mutual relationship may be considered none the less as 'conjugal' in view of our final ends. The soul itself is virtually spiritual, being no less than a projection of the Spirit into the psychic domain from which it will be, normally speaking, reabsorbed into its transcendent source. The 'glorious body of the resurrection' is so named because the body is at that moment in the process of being reabsorbed into the soul, and with the soul, by sublimation, into the Spirit.

Virtually equivalent to the polarity Spirit/soul, but less unequal and more horizontal, is the pair Heart and soul which may be said to comprise the whole human individuality. The Heart, which is the microcosmic Fountain of Life, is the gateway to the Spirit and as such it transcends the soul in the way that the centre transcends the circumference, though from a certain point of view they are at the same level of existence. The soul itself has likewise two poles: 'As all active knowledge belongs to the masculine side of the soul, and all passive being to its feminine side, thought-dominated (and therefore clearly delimited) consciousness can in a certain sense be ascribed to the masculine pole, while all involuntary powers and capacities connected with life as such appear as an expression of the feminine side'.[2]

The harmonious reunion of these two poles of the psychic substance is termed in alchemy the chemical marriage, and it is a preliminary step in the direction of 'the mystical marriage', that higher union by which the soul is reunited with the Spirit and thus regains all that was lost at the Fall. 'The marriage of the masculine and feminine forces finally merges into the marriage of Spirit and soul, and as the Spirit is the "Divine in the human"—as is written in the *Corpus Hermeticum*—this last union is related to the mystical marriage. Thus one state merges into another. The realization of the fullness of the soul leads to the abandonment of the soul to Spirit, and thus the alchemical symbols have a multiplicity of interpretations. Sun and Moon can represent the two powers of the soul (Sulphur and Quicksilver); at the same time they are the symbols of Spirit and soul.'[3]

The subdivisions are endless: each faculty of the soul may be said to have two aspects, active and passive, masculine and feminine. The same applies at all lower levels: the body is one but it has two ears, two eyes, two nostrils, two lips, two arms and two legs. Every separate thing is a unity penetrated by duality: a single flower comprises a central 'eye' and a circumference of petals, by which it symbolizes, on the human plane, the individual as such, that is, the polarity Heart-soul.

In some cases of symbolic duality it is a question of two entities becoming isolated from a larger group. There are more than two elements, but fire and water none the less form a pair which is one of the great symbols of complementarity. Analogously, amongst the five senses, sight and hearing form a distinct pair that is comparable to fire and water. It is in the nature of sound to spread, and listening involves, for the aural faculty, a dilation that induces an expansion of the whole psychic substance in receptivity. On the other hand sight concentrates itself—and with itself the soul—upon the object of vision.

The senses and what they sense are particular modes of a duality which is always with us and which concerns each one of us at every moment of consciousness. This is the pair subject-object. As we have seen, the complementary pairs may be termed male and female, active and passive, dynamic and static, or contractive and expansive. Each of these two-fold designations is analogous to the others, though each may be more immediately apt with regard to one particular pair. It is evident that the subject and the object are respectively active and passive, dynamic and static. They can also be termed male and female, but in this connection let it be remarked once again that every single thing in existence, therefore every pole of a duality, is bound to have in itself two complementary aspects. In the case of the conjugal pair, each of the two will always be the subject in respect of his or her 'male' dynamic and active pole, and each will be the object in respect of his or her 'female' expansive and passive pole. Thus the woman as subject beholds the display of the man's masculinity and not its secret, not the root of his ego which, being hidden and purely subjective, could never serve as object. But she has this as it were non-feminine experience within the framework of being herself the purely feminine pole of the marriage of male and female.

To revert once more to our initial quotation, we have seen that the immediate source of duality lies in the two complementary aspects that are to be found in the Creator Himself. But this is not its primal source: neither the Name Creator nor the Dominical Name, Lord, can be placed at the level of the Pure Absolute, because of their implicit involvement with relativity, for a lord has his subjects just as a creator has his creatures. In Islamic doctrine a distinction is made between non-essential Names—such as these two and most of the others[4]—and the names of the Essence which are purely Absolute such as the Truth, the One, the Self-Sufficient, the Independent, the Living, the Holy. Analogous distinctions are made in Hinduism and other esoterisms; and if we wish to trace the pairs to their ultimate Origin and End, we must therefore go back to the Essence Itself. There could be no complementary duality inherent in the Creator without a purely Absolute Precedent. In other words the plenitude of all complementarity can only lie in the Absolute Oneness of the Divine Selfhood, and it is here, beyond the creative Principle, that the Supreme Archetype of the pairs must be sought.

A question may arise at this point in connection with subject and object, a pair which is closely related to the personal pronouns. The third of these, He (*Huwa*) is commonly used in Islam as one of the Essential Names to denote the Absolute Truth, and an equivalent use is made in Hinduism of the demonstrative 'That' (*Tad*). But it will be clear to our readers that the Archetype of the pair subject-object is, primarily, not the Essential He but the Essential I-Thou. We say primarily because the first and second persons belong to each other and readily merge into oneness, whereas the third person has always been of indispensable value to theology as a means of expressing the Divine Incomparability and it has, for our minds, a powerful primary association with the idea of otherness.

The Supreme Subject is the Absolute in His Pure Selfhood. But the Absolute could not possibly be deprived of an object, nor could the I-Thou relationship exist as the vehicle of love throughout the universe if it were absent from That which is the Source of all things. In other words, it is a metaphysical necessity that the Divine Selfhood should possess intrinsically, as complement to the subjective Secret, an objective mode of display, and this is Infinitude. Nor can there be any particular aspect of joy or wonderment in any subject-object relationship whatsoever which does not have its archetypal plenitude in the Absolute-Infinite Oneness.

Here lies the highest meaning of the Far-Eastern symbol *Yin-Yang* which ranks with the Seal of Solomon as one of the most powerfully expressive figures of complementarity. The Absolute is white whereas the Infinite, so often symbolized by night, is black; as to their Oneness, apart from the unity of the figure as a whole, the black circle in the centre of *Yang* signifies the Infinite as an intrinsic dimension of the Absolute, and the white circle in the centre of *Yin* signifies the Absolute as an intrinsic dimension of the Infinite. Oneness of Union is also expressed in the mutual attraction between *Yang* and *Yin*, inasmuch as each has something which the other lacks and without which it cannot be complete. Like the Seal, this figure also has its applications at every level of the universe and, in a vertical sense, at two different levels.

What then of the third person? Absolute-Infinite Oneness excludes the possibility that there should be anything 'other' than Itself. But otherness is not the only signification of he, she or it, which can be used to express that which the first and second persons possess in common; and this is its original sense, that is, what it signifies in the Oneness of the Absolute I-Thou. A more precise answer to the question here raised may be deduced from the following formulation: 'God is Absolute, and being the Absolute, He is likewise the Infinite; being the Absolute and the Infinite, intrinsically and without duality, He is also the Perfect'.[5] Perfection is thus what the Absolute is conscious of sharing with the Infinite and what the Infinite is conscious of sharing with the Absolute; and since there is no duality, and therefore no separation or division between the Subject and the Object of Consciousness, Reality may be expressed in either subjective or objective terms, which gives rise to He or That as an alternative to I. Selfconsciousness is fraught with the implicit question 'What am I?', which could also be worded as a self-addressed 'What art thou?' At the highest level the answer 'I am (or Thou art, or we are) Absolute Infinite Perfection' or simply 'I am That', or 'I am It' which becomes in Islam 'I am He'[6], for want of a neuter in Arabic. The Qur'ān says *there is no god but I* and *there is no god but He*, and there is a constant easy fluctuation between the first and the third persons, when used of God, throughout the revealed book.

As the Supreme Archetype of the pairs, Absolute Infinite Perfection may be conceived of as a single Perfection that is mysteriously endowed with two aspects, as in the Taoist perspective. But it is also possible, as we shall see in the next chapter, to consider this threefold term as expressive of the Supreme Archetype of all the triads in existence.

# The Symbolism of the Triad of Primary Colours

There are certain ternaries in the world which may be called true triads in that they are irreducible to any other number except the unity from which all multiplicity proceeds. The three terms, all of the same kind and at the same level of existence, form together a harmonious totality, and each is needed by the other two in the sense that its absence would leave a gap and disrupt the equilibrium. The primary colours are an outstanding example of veritable threeness which cannot be reduced to two. Take away red, and the perfect balance would be broken in the direction of too much cold; the absence of blue would make for excessive heat; without yellow, the residue would be too ponderous.

This triad of colours may be said to affirm the truth of all the true triads which transcend it, in the way that a symbol is a 'proof' of its archetype. One of these archetypes *in divinis* is the Christian Trinity. Another, at the same degree of relative Absoluteness is the Hindu ternary of the three aspects of *Īshvara*, the Divine Personality. These aspects are *Sat-Chit-Ananda*, Being-Consciousness-Beatitude. Hinduism is particularly explicit with regard to the inevitable effect of this unmanifested triplicity upon all that lies beneath it. According to the doctrine, everything in the manifested universe—in monotheistic terms, every created thing—partakes in varying degrees of three *gunas*, that is, qualities or tendencies, and these are *sattva*, *rajas* and *tamas*. *Sattva* denotes a luminous quality and an upward tendency; *rajas* is the *guna* of expansive horizontal growth; and it is the dark and heavy *tamas* which induces ignorance and inertia and which, in a more positive sense, enables night to succeed day and guarantees, on the material plane, the operation of the law of gravity.

*Sattva* is said to be white, *rajas* red, *tamas* black, and this description is instructive. White and black which are not strictly speaking colours, symbolize the extreme contrast between *sattva* and *tamas*;[1] colour, which lies between these two poles, thus symbolizes *rajas*, the intermediary *guna*; and red may be taken to stand for colour in general because it is, of all colours, the most vivid, that is, it produces the maximum of vibrations in the eye. We cannot help noticing however that unlike the *gunas* themselves, white, red and black do not constitute a true triad. The point of view which assigns them to the *gunas* would seem to be above all methodic, which means that the approach is subjective or anthropocentric rather than objective, mystical rather than cosmological. We are in the domain of practical theology rather than that of universal symbolism. The symbolic element is there, as we have seen. But we are not being told that white, red and black owe their existence to the same transcendent threefold archetype as that which is the source of the *gunas*; we are being given the imperative injunction: count *sattva* as white and *tamas* as black—imperative because for one who is seeking to escape from the chain of samsaric births and deaths, *sattva* is precisely the means of escape, and must therefore be considered as pure positive, whereas for opposite reasons, black is needed to bring home to us the negativity of *tamas*. In a somewhat parallel way the Qur'ān addresses men and jinn as '*ye heavy ones*' (LV:31) in the sense that they are psychic rather than spiritual; and in respect of this limitation the human being does not stand in any such need of weight as might give *tamas* a positive significance from his point of view, that is, from the point of view of a fallen soul that is cut off from direct contact with the Spirit.

In order to consider the question of colour more objectively, let us revert once again to the level of the Principles themselves, without confining ourselves to Hinduism and Christianity. In the ancient Persian, Egyptian and Greco-Roman religions gold, therefore yellow, was unanimously held to be sacred to Mithras, Horus and Apollo respectively. We may note also in this connection that Ovid speaks of *flava*[2] *Minerva*; and she, in Greek Pallas Athene, born fully armed form the head of Zeus, is in a sense parallel to Apollo as a personification of the Divine Consciousness or Intelligence.[3] By analogy, albeit at a more transcendent level,[4] the luminous colour must therefore be assigned to the Second Person of the Christian Trinity, as also to *Chit* in the corresponding Hindu Ternary.

As to red, its symbolism partly coincides with that of fire, and fire has over light a certain priority[5] which is suggestive of the priority of the First Person of the Trinity over the Second, the more so in that light is 'of one substance' with fire. It is significant that for Moses the first sign of the presence of Jehovah was the burning bush; and at Mount Sinai *the Lord descended upon it in fire* (Exodus, XX:18). For the Romans red was associated with Jupiter, and in Greek the name Zeus is closely related to words which have the sense of life, heat, and fire. According to St. Clement, Zeus was considered the supreme God 'on account of his igneous nature'.[6]

The colour blue was sacred to Juno, whose Greek name Hera is etymologically related to 'air', an element which may be said to have the colour of the sky. Her bird, the peacock, makes an overall impression of blue. In Christian iconography blue is especially associated with the Blessed Virgin, one of whose titles is *Regina Caeli,* Queen of Heaven, and who 'incarnates', as it were, the Holy Ghost[7] whence, according to certain Gnostics, the 'femininity' of the Third Person of the Trinity.[8] Moreover the Virgin is not only *Regina Caeli* but also *Stella Maris*, Star of the Sea; and there is a partial symbolic coincidence between blue and water as between red and fire. According to the Persians, the Word was created by the union of the primal Fire and the primal Water,[9] and there is analogy, if not identity, between this and the Hindu ternary *Purusha*, *Prakriti* and *Buddhi*, and also that of the opening of Genesis: *And the Spirit of God moved upon the face of the waters. And God said, Let there be light.* As one of a triad, the Spirit here has its archetype in the First Person of the Trinity, the Waters in the Third and the Light in the Second.

As to the Trinity as such, it would be impossible to speak of its Three Persons if they were not prefigured in the Divine Essence Itself. As Frithjof Schuon has remarked: 'Infinitude and Perfection (or the Sovereign Good) are the intrinsic dimensions of the Absolute'. He also says: 'The Absolute is Infinite; therefore It radiates and in radiating It projects Itself, the content of this projection being the Good. The Absolute could neither radiate nor produce thereby the image of the Good if It were not in Itself, in Its Immutability, both the Good and Radiation, or in other words if It did not possess these intrinsic dimensions'.[10] This means that the Supreme Archetype of the Trinity lies in the Absolute Infinite Perfection of the Essence. The First Person is rooted in the Absolute, the Second in the Sovereign Good, and the Third in the Infinite; and all true triads throughout the Universe, beyond their other symbolisms, exist above all to affirm and 'prove'—or, as the Psalms and the Qur'ān would say, to praise—the three intrinsic dimensions of Essential Reality. The triad which is our theme is particularly eloquent in this respect: it is the right of the Absolute that we should know which is its colour before we have time to think, while the Infinite has the parallel right that our thoughts should unfold in the direction of Its two great symbols, the sky and the ocean. Nor is it difficult to perceive that gold is a manifestation of the Sovereign Good or Perfection.[11]

We saw in the last chapter how another true triad, that of the three linguistic persons, reflects the Source of all triplicity.[12] We also saw how this correspondence may be reconciled with the symbolism of the pairs, all of which originate from the duality Absolute Perfection and Infinite Perfection which mysteriously underlies the Divine Oneness: Perfection may be considered as latent in both the Absolute and the Infinite or it may be 'extracted' from both as a third dimension of the One Essence. The same reconciliation between duality and triplicity may be expressed in terms of colour: if yellow remains latent in red and blue, the resultant tints of flame and turquoise make a perfect pair which altogether satisfies the eye as a self-sufficient match of complements; but the triplicity is still there, for the two colours owe the perfection of their complementarity to the presence of yellow in each.

It will now be clear, as regards the three *gunas*, that although according to practical theology they are white, red and black, the ultimate source from which these qualities or tendencies derive is symbolized in its intrinsic dimensions by the three primary colours. As reflections of Absolute Infinite Perfection, *sattva*, *rajas* and *tamas* must therefore be considered as yellow, red and blue respectively.[13] This means, at first sight somewhat paradoxically, that *sattva* results directly from *Chit* rather than from *Sat*; but the essentially 'sattvic' nature of *Chit* becomes evident if we bear in mind that It is, precisely, *Sat's* Self-Consciousness of Perfection.[14] In Christian terms the same truth could be expressed by saying that the whole message of the Logos, the Divine Word, is summed up in the precept: 'Be ye perfect, even as your Father in Heaven is Perfect'.

*Sat*, which corresponds to the Trinity's First Person, is reflected at every level of the manifested universe by *rajas* which is, as we have seen, of the 'colour' of the Absolute. Whereas the Infinite is mirrored in time and space and other more transcendent modes of duration and extent, and whereas Perfection is the source of the qualitative aspects of things, the Absolute is responsible for a thing's existence, as opposed to its non-existence, and existence may be said to include growth.[15] This is precisely the domain of *rajas* which ensure expansive development at a given level and which is not concerned with either upward or downward movement.

Just as *Sat* is the first determination of the Absolute, so *Ananda*, Beatitude, which corresponds to the Third Person of the Trinity, is the first determination of the Infinite. We may quote here yet again the all-important Islamic Tradition: *I was a Hidden Treasure and I loved to be known and so I created the world*; and we have already seen that it is the Infinite which prefigures the means of this outward radiation. Blue, its colour, is therefore also the colour of extent and of distance, which in itself is a blessed liberation.[16] It is to this aspect of distance that the vault of heaven bears witness. But when outward manifestation reaches a certain stage, its aspect of freedom inevitably changes to limitation and danger, at any rate in respect of fallen man. Distance, for him, takes on the negative aspect of remoteness from God, and the movement away from the Principle is a current of degeneration that must be resisted. From this standpoint it would be inopportune and misleading to describe *tamas*[17] as blue. It has to be thought of as black, with a saving opposite of white.

To revert once more to distance in its positive sense, far-sightedness of breadth of vision may be counted as a subjective aspect of it. Moreover blue is the cold colour and therefore the colour of impartiality and objectivity. All these qualities make it clear why blue is universally one of the greatest symbols of Truth and of Wisdom. It is also a symbol of Eternity, which is one with Truth inasmuch as that which is True or Real is that which can never pass away. This aspect of Truth is reflected in the static quality of blue as compared with the more volatile red and yellow; and by extension from Eternity, as the colour of immortality, blue plays a large part in many different traditions in connection with the dead in varying ways—amulets placed in the tomb, hearse-cloths, shrouds and the like.[18] Another projection of Eternal Truth is the virtue of constancy or fidelity, whence the mediaeval and still current phrase 'true blue'; and as the colour of depth, blue has not only an adamantine firmness but also an aspect of unfathomability in virtue of which it is a symbol of the Divine Mystery, the Secret (*as-Sirr*) as it is termed in Sufism. For the Taoists in particular, blue symbolizes the inscrutable nature of Tao.[19]

Nothing that is below the Divine Essence can fail to reflect, in some degree or other, Its Absolute Infinite Perfection, and we have already seen how this ternary appears at the level of the Personal God as *Sat-Chit-Ananda*. At the next level in the hierarchy, which marks the outset of manifestation, *Buddhi*, the created Logos, has a triple manifestation, *Trimūrti*,[20] whose persons are Brahmā,[21] Vishnu and Shiva. The same triplicity is expressed in Christianity in the formulation *I am the Way, the Truth and the Life*. As the exteriorisation of *Īshvara* in his aspect of *Sat*, *Brahmā* is the productive principle of manifested beings. He therefore corresponds to 'the Life', with *rajas* as his *guna* and red as his colour. *Vishnu* exteriorises *Chit* and fulfils the function of Logos in the strict sense. He corresponds to 'the Way' with *sattva* as his *guna* and yellow[22] as his colour. *Shiva*, who exteriorises *Ananda* and thereby the Infinite, is the transforming principle, which means that he is *a priori* the power that terminates existences[23] on lower planes with a view to their regeneration. He corresponds to 'the Truth',[24] with *tamas* as his *guna* and blue as his colour or black, according to the standpoint.

Since the religions are manifestations of the Divine Word, let us consider in this same context the triad of monotheistic religions which have been said to correspond, in the order of their revelation, to the Three Persons of the Trinity. They are also said, in Sufism, to correspond to the three great principles of spirituality, namely to fear, love and knowledge;[25] and there is an analogy between these principles and the Hindu ways of action, love and knowledge.[26] Judaism may be termed a path of action because its very substance consists of a multitude of ritual acts accomplished in obedience to a strict and complex law which covers every aspect of life. It goes without saying that each of the monotheisms is a self-sufficient, totally independent whole, and that it is therefore representative of each of the three terms of all the triads we are considering here. But there are none the less questions of stress, apart from a certain continuity and development between the three faiths; and it is to Judaism, the first, that we owe the formulation *Fear of the Lord is the beginning of wisdom* (Ps. III: 10), an axiom with which the religion of Moses is deeply penetrated. Now red, the colour of the Divine Majesty, is by extension expressive of justice and of danger. It may thereby be considered the colour of fear; and as the essentially dynamic colour, it is likewise the colour of action.

We have seen, with reference to the Old Testament, the connection between fire, therefore red, and Jehovah. But it might be objected that the religion that is named after the Second Person of the Trinity has also a powerful claim on red which, in addition to its other significations,[27] is a symbol of love. This is true, and it has already been admitted that each religion has necessarily a claim on all the colours. But apart from the fact that yellow is also the symbol of love, in particular of Divine love,[28] what distinguishes Christianity above all from the other two religions in question is the manifestation of the Divinity, the living presence of God, and manifestation is of the colour of light. Thus in Hinduism the guarantors of the maintenance of religion throughout the cycle of four ages, namely the ten Avatāras (Divine descents), are incarnations, not of Brahmā or Shiva, but of the yellow-robed Vishnu; and the followers of the *bhakti-marga*, the way of love, are generally known as *Vaishnava* (Vishnuites). It is moreover in the nature of things that the Divine Presence should be the source of a perspective of love.

By contrast Christ predicted for Islam a perspective dependent upon the *Spirit of Truth which proceedeth from the Father* (John XV:26). The difference between it and the Christian outlook is also implicit in the words: *I have yet many things to say unto you but ye cannot bear them now. Howbeit when he, the Spirit of truth, is come, he will guide you into all truth* (John XVI:12-13).[29] The Gospels are, as it were, wrapped round the person of Jesus. The perspective of love does not tolerate too much looking to the right or the left, but the Qur'ān demands on the contrary that one should look well in all directions *for wheresoever ye turn, there is the face of God* (II:115). This change from 'yellow' to 'blue' was in the nature of things, for there is an obvious connection between Truth and old age, the time of life that is normally characterized by serene objectivity, and Islam is the religion of the old age of the cycle, the threshold of the meeting of extremes, death and regeneration, of which Shiva is the Lord. Nor could Sufism, Islamic mysticism, be other than a way of knowledge; and it may be noted in this respect that the Divine Essence is often addressed by the Sufis as Layla, a woman's name which has the meaning of night. In this highest sense, night is the symbol of Absolute Reality in its 'feminine' aspect of Infinitude. The blue-black night sky with its stars reflects the 'womb' of Infinite Totality in which the supreme archetypes of all existing things are mysteriously contained in Oneness.

The Qur'ān is called the Book of Truth, and it can also be called the Book of Mercy inasmuch as all its chapters but one begin with the words *In the Name of God, the Infinitely Good and Boundlessly Merciful*. The identity of Infinitude and Mercy is affirmed in the verse *My Mercy embraceth all things* (VII:156). The first of these two Names of Mercy, *ar-Raḥmān*, is related to the Name *al-Muḥīt*, the All-Embracing; and this word has by extension the meaning of ocean. Like the blue sky and the blue cloak of the Virgin, the seas (*maria* in Latin) inasmuch as they surround the land are a symbol of Infinite Mercy. The Name *ar-Raḥmān* could almost be translated the Infinitely Comprehending, which would serve to indicate the profound cognitive connection, not obvious at first sight, between Mercy and Truth, both of which are symbolized by the same colour.

The second Name of Mercy, *ar-Raḥīm*, the Boundlessly Merciful, is also by extension a name of the Prophet. Whereas the first Name denotes the Divine Source of Mercy, this second Name is expressive of all manifested Mercy; and here lies the explanation why green is generally considered to be the colour of Islam. Yellow is the colour of manifestation, and if it be brought to bear upon blue the result is green. The Qur'ān speaks of the green garments worn by blessed souls in Paradise, and Paradise itself, symbolized by the oases in the desert, and named in Arabic 'the Garden', is always thought of as verdant. But if this compound colour[30] stands for the religion as such, there is no doubt that by a typically Islamic ellipsis—for Islam loves to dwell on the roots of things—blue rather than green is the dominant colour of Islamic art. More than one famous mosque is known as the Blue Mosque, while there are very many others to which this name might well be given; and in Qur'ān manuscripts, apart from the illuminators' evident love of blue, there seems to be an unwritten law that wherever sections of text or ornamentation are framed within borders, the outermost border shall be blue, as if in illustration of the above quoted verse *My Mercy embraceth all things.*

Needless to say, these general considerations lay themselves open to many apparent inconsistencies which can however be explained away if we bear in mind that everything is bound to partake of all the three intrinsic dimensions of the Supreme Reality, even though it be eminently representative of one of them in particular. We have seen for example that red is traditionally associated with Jupiter and blue with Juno. But if she is Queen of Heaven, he, for his part, is King of Heaven, and as such he also has a claim on the colour of the firmament. Astrologically speaking, blue corresponds to his planet, the greater benefic, whereas green corresponds to Venus, the lesser benefic; and the parts played in Virgil's *Aeneid* by the two deities who give their names to these planets are analogous to the functions of the two Names of Mercy in Arabic which we have just been considering and of which the same two colours are symbols.

To take another example, Krishna is the eighth Avatāra of Vishnu, and as such he is invariably depicted as robed in a yellow garment, but nonetheless as being in himself of the colours of Shiva, and this is indicated in his name. The explanation is no doubt that the ninth Avatāra was the founder of Buddhism, whereas the tenth will have a universal function that concerns all religions. Krishna is thus, for this cycle of time, the last Divine descent on behalf of Hinduism; and it is in perfect accordance with his finality that within the framework of Vishnu he should be representative of Shiva. This is borne out by the *Bhagavadgita*, the Song of the Lord, namely of Krishna, for its perspective is Shivaite rather than Vishnuite.

Leaving the reader to resolve other apparent contradictions along similar lines, let us, in conclusion, dwell briefly once more on the supreme symbolic significance of the triad which is our theme. Very relevant to this is a note by Frithjof Schuon, in his previously quoted *From the Divine to the Human*, on Beyond-Being which, as we have seen, he defines as Absolute Infinite Perfection. The note is partly necessitated by the unwillingness of Christian theologians in general to raise their intelligences above the level of the Trinity. 'Concerning the transcendence of Beyond-Being, it is necessary to emphasize that in reality this transcendence is absolute plenitude, so that it could not possibly have a privative meaning: to say that the Trinity is surpassed therein means, not that the Trinity is abolished in its essentials, but that it is comprised—and prefig-

ured in respect of its ontological or hypostatic projection—
in Beyond-Being in a way which, while being undifferentiated, is eminently positive; in the same way as the Vedantic
Sat-Chit-Ananda which, though it corresponds to an already relative vision, is none the less ineffably and
supereminently comprised in the pure absoluteness of
Atmā'.[31]

What is said here of the Christian Trinity and its Hindu
equivalent can and must be said of the primary colours. To
suppose that their ultimate undifferentiated Oneness simply means that they are, as it were, absorbed into white
would be a most misleading simplification. Such a reduction to unity would be an abolution of the essentials of
colour, and it would therefore be a privation altogether out
of keeping with the plenitude of Beyond-Being. The colours
are given us in this world to bear witness to the wealth of
the 'Hidden Treasure' and to affirm precisely that it is not
'monotonous' in any negative sense. Among the essentials
of red, yellow and blue is their harmonious contrast. The
word 'ineffably' in the above quotation is altogether to the
point, for we are here beyond the limits of what the mind
can conceive and what the tongue can express. It is a contradiction in terms that there should be any room for con-
trasts in undifferentiated Oneness. But it is well known in
more than one mysticism that the perplexity[32] caused by
certain apparent contradictions can be a basis for intellection. In other words it can serve as a stepping stone from
the mind to the Heart, for the Heart can intuit what the
brain cannot think. The Qur'ān tells us: *And whatsoever
He hath created for you on earth of diverse hues, verily
wherein is a sign for people bent on remembrance*
(XVI:13). The reference here is clearly to the 'Platonic'
remembrance of a Divine Archetype, the remembrance

which a sign or symbol of that Archetype has power to awaken in the higher reaches of the intelligence.

It is said in Sufism that knowledge of the Truth entails the grasping of 'the union of opposites'.[33] Adapted to our immediate context, this means the certitude that the piercing distinctnesses which delight us in colour are not obliterated in the Oneness, but that on the contrary they are to be seen there, and there only, in all the fullness of their divergence. This doctrine is moreover latent in the symbol itself, for to see a colour at its purest and best, as one does sometimes in a flower, is to see an imprint of the Absolute which guarantees that the beatific vision in the highest sense will not fail to reveal the Eternal Origin of that particular aesthetic experience. When the Qur'ān says *There is nothing that doth not praise Him* (XVII:44), it authorizes us to say when we see a colour, singly or with others: 'If this be merely the shadow, Glory to the Substance!' The colours are bearers, from their Supreme Source, of the message: 'Beware of estimating my Infinite Beauty according to the poverty of mental conceptions of My Oneness'.

## CHAPTER FIVE

# The Archetypes of Devotional Homage

What man's human nature stands in need of above everything else is the transcendent spiritual nature which opens
it to the Absolute. Failing that, inasmuch as his fallen human nature no longer has access to the Heart, the gateway
of the Spirit, what he most needs is faith, and all that faith
implies in the way of religion with its doctrine and practice. But if in addition, on the basis of this foremost re-
quirement, we were to assess the priorities of his other
earthly needs, that of a consort would no doubt rank among
the first. It is not for nothing that the Prophet of Islam said:
'Marriage is half the religion'. Filial and parental relationships, also psychologically needed, are subordinate to the
central conjugal relationship, but like it they are projections or manifestations of Divinity, inasmuch as parent and
offspring have their supra-celestial archetypes in the Creator and the Divine Word respectively. As to the fraternal
relationship, together with friendship which may be considered as its prolongation, these likewise spring from an
Uncreated Source, as we shall see. The perfect fulfillment
of all the reciprocal possibilities so far mentioned is promised for Paradise, whereas in this life that perfection may
or may not be distinctly foreshadowed. There is another
relationship which, like these, can only be consummated
in the Hereafter, but which, for its earthly foretaste, is less
subject to the hazards of destiny, thanks to religion. The
need it meets is the thirst, universal to man, for contact on

the earthly plane with an outstanding representative of perfection, that is, with the personification of an ideal. But before enlarging on this, let us consider more fully the nature of man.

We can take as our starting point the Chinese character *wang* which means king, or more precisely, king-pontiff.[1] It consists of three horizontal lines one above the other, the middle line being crossed by a vertical which just touches, at its two extremities, the highest and the lowest horizontals, and which traces out man's mediation between Heaven and earth. The character's central section alone would suffice in fact to figure the meaning of *wang*—witness the Christian cross which has that significance amongst many others. Nonetheless, the additional horizontals at the head and the foot of the cross serve respectively to denote the pontiff's two natures, heavenly and earthly, and to indicate that there can be no effective mediation between two worlds if one does not truly belong to both. In Christianity the epithet 'very', that is, 'true' is doctrinally applied to each of the two natures of Christ; and the necessity of his being 'very man' is to be asked why God had not sent an Angel instead of Muhammad to found the religion of Islam: *If there were on earth angels walking at their ease, We had sent down upon them an angel as messenger* (XVII:95). The words *at their ease* could be somewhat freely rendered 'in their element' or 'at home'. The Angels can visit earth, but they can never belong to earth, whereas to be fully man presupposes two sets of preoccupations, one with the therebeyond and the other with the herebelow.

Ever since the primordial pre-religious age it is the founders and renewers of religion who have most amply fulfilled the function of king-pontiff, and it is they who have been the most outstanding objects of what is called devotional homage or hero-worship, though this does not preclude the existence of countless lesser objects of such devotion in a variety of lesser degrees. But although in the case of the Prophets and the Saints the prophethood or sanctity of the hero is an essential factor in the background of the relationship which is our theme, it is not the immediate object of attachment. The veneration in question cannot be disassociated from the earthly nature of its object. There is something in such a commitment which proceeds from soul to soul, and it is necessary that the 'worshipped' should be, or have been, at the same level of existence as the 'worshipper', faced by the same conditions and having therefore in a very general way the same basic elementary concerns to which all life on earth is subject.

It is true that such devotion does not lend itself to analysis, and it could be said that the difficulty of enclosing it within definite lines of demarcation increases in proportion to the eminence of its object, above all when the hero is also the recipient of worship in the higher and normal sense of the term, or even beyond it. The names of Jesus, the Buddha and Krishna, for example, may be invoked as names of the Absolute, while on the other hand certain aspects of their lives on earth may be taken as models for imitation; but there is likely to be, in the case of such examples as those just given, a medial region where one kind of devotion overlaps with another; and in any case the Absolute is always ultimately the magnet of attraction, whatever the level of Its manifestation.

The extreme amplitude of the exemplars just given and of their peers is brought out with great clarity by Frithjof Schuon in his comparison of the Saint who is not a Prophet with those who have, in addition to their sanctity, the cosmic function of what Buddhists call the Bodhisattva, the Saint who is destined for Buddhahood, that is, for a function equal to that of a major Avatāra of Hinduism, or a founder of religion in the domain of monotheism. As regards exaltation the fully realized Saint is not to be surpassed, since in Gnosis the Knower and the Known are One; but the 'horizontal' radiation of Sainthood in the normal sense, though necessarily great, is not to be compared with 'the unimaginable cosmic deployment of the perfection of the Bodhisattva'.[2]

In the Qur'ān the Prophet is told: *Verily of an immense magnitude is thy nature* (LXVIII:4). He is also told, with reference to the tremendous impact of Revelation, which only such magnitude as his would be capable of enduring: *If We had sent down this Qur'ān upon a mountain, thou wouldst have seen it lying prostrate in humility, rent asunder through fear of God* (LIX:21). Referring in more general terms to the qualification to bear such a burden, which amounts to no less than the capacity to conceive and bring forth a whole world, that is, a religion together with the theocratic civilization which necessarily evolves from it, Schuon writes: 'Far from tending exclusively towards the non-manifested, the angelic humanity of the virtual Buddha radiates on the contrary throughout the cosmos as the sun lights up the darkness of night. It is this, we repeat, which makes it capable of acting as vehicle for that crystallisation of the Infinite which Revelation is, seed and sustenance of a universal and millennial tradition'.[3]

As an equivalent to 'that crystallisation of the Infinite' he also defines Revelation as 'that Truth made flesh' to include more explicitly those cases where the Divine message comes as a man rather than as 'the Word made book'; and he expressly mentions the Virgin Mary as exemplifying the capacity we are speaking of, an amplitude which, as he points out, is not part of the function of great Saints such a Ramakrishna and Ramana Maharshi who may none the less be her equals in exaltation, that is, in Gnosis. Of her radiance on the 'horizontal' plane he writes: 'This supereminent perfection was indispensable for her function as "co-redemptress", but such an endowment is a providential disposition or a cosmic prodigality which, while necessarily being accompanied from a certain moment by Knowledge, does not have to be there in order that Knowledge may be obtained. If it did, it would be useless to talk about Gnosis and to teach it to ordinary mortals'.[4]

The Qur'ān speaks of Jesus and his mother as *a sign for the worlds* (XXI:91); and the breadth of every such perfection is partly to be measured by the reaction produced by its presence in the cosmos. Despite the differences of religious perspectives there is a remarkable sameness of reaction the world over, the same great cause being always identifiable in its corresponding effect, in a devotion which is, of its kind, incomparable for its intensity, diffusion and endurance, and which remains undiminished even if, as is the case with regard to Muhammad and to Mary, the religion forbids it to cross the boundary line which separates devotional homage from worship in the ordinary sense.

In view of what was initially said about the thirst for contact on the earthly plane with perfection personified, it might be argued that the preceding paragraphs about persons no longer situated in this world have taken us somewhat away from our subject. But an aspect of 'the unimaginable cosmic deployment' of all the examples given is its triumph over death and over time and space. The religions in question have continued throughout the centuries to draw vitality from the as it were still living presence of those who presided over their foundation. It is true that the immediate companions of the Prophets are always counted as having been exceptionally blessed; but another feature

of the 'cosmic deployment' we are speaking of is to provide certain compensations for later generations whose lives
did not coincide with that of the great central hero of their
perspective. At the outset of a religion its sacred arts are
still no more than seeds in the soul of its founder; their
flowering plays a part in the perpetuation of the presence
of that soul: to stand outside or inside a great cathedral, for
example, can be to encounter mysteriously the person of
Jesus.

To take another example of enduring presence, let us
quote once more from Frithjof Schuon. The reference,
needless to say, is to places where—over fifty years ago—
the Islamic civilisation still remained intact, as yet
unpenetrated by the modern world: 'On our first visits to
Arab towns we were impressed by the austere and even
sepulchral atmosphere: a kind of whiteness of the desert
was spread like a shroud over houses and people; everywhere there was a breath of prayer and of death. In this we
see beyond question a trace of the soul of the Prophet'.[5]

To be mediator between Heaven and earth is not the
ultimate function of man; and since Paradise will have the
last word, it is not illegitimate to give it, on occasion, the
first word also. We can thus define the herebelow nature of
man as an immortal soul made for Paradise and therefore
capable of spiritualisation, but temporarily exiled to earth,
and a body made for Paradise and therefore capable of
resurrection and transubstantiation but also temporarily
exiled to earth where, like the soul, it is allowed to anticipate remotely some of the experiences destined for it in
Paradise. If man is ephemerally mediator between Heaven
and earth, he is everlastingly mediator between the Absolute and the relative, or between the Absolute in Itself and
the Absolute in the relative, or between a higher and a lower
Paradise. Given the duality which underlies man's unity, it

is in the nature of things that two Paradises should be required to satisfy his aspirations. The Qur'ān promises two for each blessed soul, and it mentions two pairs of Celestial Gardens at different levels (LV:46, 62). According to one of the most frequently quoted commentaries[6] the higher pair consists of the Paradise of the Essence and the Paradise of the Spirit. Each Garden is characterised by its fruit, and of the fruits mentioned with reference to the two upper Gardens, namely the date and the pomegranate, the commentator says that the date belongs to the Spirit, 'for in its Paradise the kernel of the individuality still remaineth', whereas the pomegranate conforms to the nature of the Essence which admits of no such individual residue. Analogously, as regards the two lower Gardens, the Paradise of the Heart implies a relative extinction of the psychic individual, and its fruit is the fig, whereas the olive, which consists mostly of kernel, is the fruit of the Paradise of the Soul.

This same passage of the Qur'ān has also been commented by Frithjof Schuon.[7] In particular he brings out the analogy between the higher and the lower pairs by making a distinction in each pair between a 'horizontal' Garden and a 'vertical' Garden, which accords perfectly with Kāshāni's commentary. The Paradise of the Spirit is the abode of the differentiated persons of those who have attained to Union, and although it ranks as the summit of all created splendour, it is none the less 'horizontal' in relation to Union Itself which is the Paradise of the Essence. 'As for the two lower Gardens, the higher of the two will not be a Paradise of Union but of beatific vision, this vision being, like Union, "vertical" in relation to a "horizontal" and therefore phenomenal and specifically human beatitude'.[8] This lowest of the Gardens, the Paradise of the Soul, is the one which most immediately concerns our theme, and then, in ascending order, the other 'horizontal' Gardens[9] which lie above it. If the supreme spiritual lights must be said to have their fullest manifestation in the Paradise of the Spirit, that does not preclude their appearance at every level in the whole hierarchy of celestial abodes. Religions are unanimous that one of the beatitudes of Paradise, regardless of its degree, is the presence at its centre of one or more of those who have been, for its inmates, the objects of their greatest veneration. Nor would it be without significance to add that souls agree about this, for the longing in question is deeply ingrained in human nature, and that is a criterion, a guarantee that it corresponds to a reality.

To grasp the symbolism of the reciprocity we are considering, it is essential to understand that all devotional homage, all hero-worship worthy of the name, proceeds subjectively from the perfection which exists in every soul, even though, in the majority, it has been buried under the rubble of a fallen second nature. If the burial is too deep, the sense of values can be irremediably vitiated; but even a remote consciousness of the latent perfection is enough to serve as a basis for having ideals and to arouse in souls, at contact with actual perfection, the nostalgic recognition of a fulfilment which for themselves also is a possibility and a goal to be reached. Herebelow the relationship in question is thus virtually between a lesser and a greater perfection.

Salvation is a guarantee of virtual perfection that is capable of being actualized; but nothing less than actual perfection can enter Paradise. It could not be otherwise,[10] inasmuch as all those who pass through the gates of Heaven incur thereby a tremendous responsibility: it is henceforth the function of each to be, himself or herself, an integral feature of the celestial Garden, a source of felicity for all the other inmates, a vehicle of the Divine Presence. In the heavenly archetype of devotional homage the lesser perfection is thus an actualized perfection and not merely a virtuality as in its earthly symbol. Otherwise expressed, in the archetypal domain not only the hero but also the hero-worshipper has something of inestimable value to offer, the more so in that every perfection, lesser or greater, is unique. This must not, however, be taken in any egalitarian sense that might suggest a reduction of the intensity of the worship, for subjectively the actualization that has taken place includes the perfecting of discernment and the sense of proportions and, objectively speaking, the higher the plane the greater the disparities. *Behold how We have favoured some of them above others; and verily the hereafter is greater in degrees and greater in precedences of favouring* (Qur'ān XVII:21). None the less it must be remembered that since the formal barriers of the herebelow have been transcended, the lesser may have an intimacy with the greater such as immeasurably surpasses all terrestrial privileges.

The immense privileges resulting from such intimacy are one of the themes of *Pearl*, which is among the most remarkable of mediaeval English poems. It tells us of the visit of a bereaved father to the grave of his beloved daughter. He kneels at the graveside, and while praying for her spiritual welfare, he is overcome by sleep. In his sleep he has a dream, or rather in this case let us venture to call it a vision, in which his daughter comes to him. He asks her how she is, but any such question is superfluous, so great is the radiance of her happiness. She tells him that she is the Queen of Heaven. He expostulates with her that this is not possible inasmuch as there is only one Queen of Heaven, namely the Blessed Virgin Mary. She replies that this is indeed the case, but that such is her generosity that she allows them all to share with her the greatness of that royalty.

Not without bearing on our context are the last words which the Prophet of Islam was heard to utter,[11] 'with the supreme communion', words which are to be understood in the light of a passage from the Qur'ān which he had just quoted, *with those upon whom God hath showered His favour, the prophets and the sages*[12] *and the martyrs and the righteous, most excellent for communion are they* (IV:69). This utterance, made at the summit of the hierarchy by one of the greatest objects of devotional homage, is particularly relevant here in that it expresses his joyous presentiment of the company, in Paradise, not only of his peers but also of the lesser perfections, the least of which are those who are termed *the righteous*. The celestial archetype of hero-worship could thus be defined as a blissfully harmonious interrelation between greater and lesser perfections, each of which has something to give and something to receive. The celestial archetype of fraternity and friendship is, on the other hand, the communion of equals or near equals, between prophet and prophet, sage and sage, and between peers within other constellations of Spirits who are drawn together by their parity.

Once more with reference to the two Paradises promised to every blessed soul, it will be clear from what has already been said that the 'vertical' Garden is always the domain of worship in its highest sense, whereas it is in the 'horizontal' Garden that the different manifested perfections are interrelated. The immediate archetypes of earthly hero-worship are thus to be found in the Paradise of the Soul. But these archetypes are themselves symbols of the analogous relationships which vastly transcend them in the higher 'horizontal' Gardens, of which the highest is that of the Spirit. It is to this Paradise that the above quoted last utterance of the Prophet of Islam must be held to refer in particular, though it can also apply to Paradise as a whole in view of the constant appearances, at every level of the celestial hierarchy, of those who personify supreme holiness.

It may now be asked what the Paradise of the Spirit symbolizes in its turn, for it is not possible that this multiple beatitude should spring into existence without the warrant, above it, of a purely Divine Archetype. In his chapter on 'The Two Paradises',[13] Frithjof Schuon mentions, as parallel to the Islamic symbolism of the two Gardens, a Christian tradition according to which the elect, that is, the dwellers in the Paradise of the Spirit, will wear 'Crowns of Uncreated Light'. These Divine Crowns may be said to stand for the Supreme Garden, that of Union, and they can be identified with what Muḥyiddīn ibn al-'Arabī terms 'the Immutable Entities' (al-a'yān ath-thābitah) which are the Divine Archetypes of created beings. We have here the highest aspect of the symbolism of stars. Although day and night draw their existence from the Absolute and the Infinite respectively, day has, in its aspect of proceeding from night, a secondary meaning of manifestation,[14] and it is from this point of view that the Stellar Archetypes are to be intuited: hidden in the day of illusion, they come into their own in the Night of Reality. Thus, as we have already seen,[15] the Divine Essence, in its aspect of Infinitude, is addressed as Night, in Arabic Layla, the name of a woman and in particular of the most famous heroine of romance in the tradition of the Arabs. Qays, her lover, is better known as Majnūn (madman) because of the intensity of his love for Layla, and Islamic mysticism has as it were annexed this couple to represent allegorically the love of the Sufi for the Divinity. During the last thousand years love poems have been regularly addressed to the Divine Essence under the name of Layla, and in one such poem of this century the Shaykh Aḥmad al-'Alawī affirms his own spiritual realization in the line: 'My star resplendeth in her firmament'.[16] This Star, which is his 'Crown of Uncreated Light', is his presence in the Paradise of Union ('her firmament'). As such, it is the Immutable Entity from which he draws his existence.

If the celestial archetype of devotional homage be defined as the communion of lesser and greater perfections, then its Divine Archetype may be said to lie in the communion of the Stars on the face of the Night of the Infinitude. If on the other hand devotional homage be simply defined as marveling at perfection, then it may be said to originate, like the third personal pronoun, in the Absolute-Infinite's Consciousness of Its own Perfection. The equivalence of these two Archetypes is revealed in Ibn al 'Arabī's brief poem on the Immutable Entities as our Origin and our End:

> We were letters, exalted, not yet uttered,
> Held aloft in the keep of the Highest of Summits.
> I therein am Thou, and we are Thou,
> And Thou art He, and all is in He-is-He—
> Ask of any that so far hath reached.[17]

Referring back to the promised paradisal intimacy between devotees and the objects of their devotion, it may be deduced from the above lines that those intimacies are necessary as a bridge, a prefiguration of union. Reality is One, and worship is a dualism which has to be transcended. In other words, every utterance of devotion is rooted in a hidden consciousness of identity. All worship, at whatever degree, must be ultimately absorbed into the Absolute, that is, into God's affirmation of Himself, *there is no god but He* and *there is no god but I.*

## CHAPTER SIX

# The Language of the Gods

The question whether or not Primordial Man can be said to have had any art is analogous to the question already asked about religion, and the answer, yes or no, depends in both cases on what exactly is meant by religion and art. If he had no religion, then he had no art, and needed no art, just as he needed no religion in the remedial sense of the word. None the less it has often been said that the movements of our first ancestors had the beauty of dance and that their speech was poetry; and Frithjof Schuon writes: 'Man is, by his theomorphism, both work of art and artist: work of art because he is an "image" and artist because this image is that of the Divine Artist'.[1] He adds in a note: 'God is, according to Masonic language, "The Great Architect of the Universe", but He is also painter, sculptor, musician, poet; according to a certain Hindu symbolism, He creates and destroys the worlds "by dancing".'

From this vaster standpoint a human work of art can be defined as anything that is made or done by man in some degree of consciousness that he is the representative on earth of the Supreme Artist—a degree high enough to ensure the absence of any individualistic opacity between the Divine Beauty and the masterpieces which result from Its radiation. Nor will it be irrelevant to quote here a remark of Schuon's about 'more or less primordial man', that is, man who is 'not too marked by the Fall': 'The gait of the human being is as evocative as his vertical posture;

whereas the animal is horizontal and only advances towards itself—that is, it is enclosed within its own form—man, in advancing, transcends himself; even his forward movement seems vertical, it denotes a pilgrimage towards his Archetype, towards the celestial Kingdom'.[2] This has, it is true, the pure spontaneity which art in the narrower technical sense excludes, for even the extemporizations of the traditional artist presuppose a deliberately chosen framework and a basis of rules. None the less, it might well be affirmed that some of the postures and movements of sacred dance must have been anticipated by primordial postures and movements.

As to primordial speech, that likewise cannot be called an art in the narrower sense. But let us dwell for a moment on the question of language, since poetry, no doubt the oldest of arts, opens the way to some general considerations which our theme will not allow us to pass over in silence.

It must be remembered that man, as first created, was fully endowed with intellectual intuition; in him the Fall had not yet obstructed the flow of remembrance from symbol to Archetype. There is consequently no fundamental difference between the Quranic doctrine that God taught Adam the names of things (II:31) and the verse of Genesis which tells us that God brought His creatures to Adam *to see what he would name them* (II:19). The two scriptures differ simply inasmuch as Genesis is here the more fully informative in telling us that language came to Adam not by any outward revelation through the intermediary of an Archangel but through a no less Providential inward intellection. Both scriptures affirm, for Adam, a God-vouchsafed authority to give each thing its name, which amounts to saying that these names, far from being arbitrary, were the phonations that exactly corresponded to what they expressed, echoes or symbols of the verbal archetypes that are the means of celestial converse. The words first used to convey man's thought were thus divinely apt. It would therefore not be inappropriate to entitle primordial speech 'the language of the Gods'.[3] What then, it may be asked, of the universal dictum that 'poetry is the language of the Gods'? Are we obliged to refute that dictum, given that none of the summits of poetic art known to us are in the long-forgotten primordial language, and many of them, no doubt most, are not even in one of the sacred languages?

This question, to which the answer is no, brings us to the main part of our chapter which is concerned with art in the narrower and more precise sense of the term as it has been used throughout historical times. It must not be forgotten that our world of symbols is relatively a domain of analysis and separation or division. No single symbol, such as the primordial language, can ever do justice to all the aspects of the great archetypal synthesis of which it is a practical manifestation, *a known measure*, as the Qur'ān says.[4] The fact that there are, throughout the world, so many different forms of the 'Supreme Name', that is, the Name of the Absolute, guaranteed by Heaven as a sacrament, is itself an argument which, all things considered, leaves no more that need be said. Let it none the less be added that in the process of the development and divergence of tongues from that of primordial man there is reason to suppose, despite certain very inferior ultimate results, that Heaven has not always allowed the current of degeneration to have a total liberty in its debasement of language. Providence has shown itself to be protective and even, at times, restorative. Moreover this may be said to apply not only to ancient times, that is, to the birth of sacred languages such as Sanskrit, Chinese, Hebrew and Arabic, and the liturgical languages such as Pali, Greek, Latin and Old Slavonic, but also to later times, even as late as the Middle Ages.[5] On the other hand, the celestial archetype of language may project echoes of itself not only in single words but in whole phrases or sentences. A line of verse, for example, may have an overwhelming beauty out of all proportion to the single words of which it is composed.

However that may be, the mention of the primordial language was not irrelevant as preamble, because it is a vehicle rather than a content, and what concerns us now is not the symbolic content of art, which is too vast a subject for a single chapter, though it will inevitably be touched on throughout the book. In speaking of symbolism and art we have in mind what might be called, for want of a better term, symbolic substance. Every masterpiece of art has two messages, one of which it possesses in common with its peers, whereas the other is more or less peculiar to itself; and it is the shared message, which is global and synthetic, that concerns us here. There is something in every such achievement, be it a summit of language or pure sound or visual beauty, which compels in us the recognition that the work in question has 'fallen from Heaven'. Our theme is expressly that aspect of art which precipitates, in the particular case of poetry, the avowal that it is 'the language of the Gods'. Nor can this supreme title be limited to poetry, inasmuch as the very qualification for any work of art to be considered in this highly exclusive context is that it should be 'divinely eloquent'. The message we are speaking of could be expressed: 'I bear witness to the Divine Beauty'—a message which cannot be faithfully delivered without the help of the Spirit, that is, without inspiration.

There can be no artistic inspiration without openness to the world of the Spirit, where dwell the mediators between man and the Divine Beauty. These vehicles of the breath of Spirit, bearers of the winds which respond to the artist's aspirations, are variously personified in the different traditions. In the Western World, Christian as well as pre-Christian, it is the Muses who are besought for help, and above all Apollo, whose identity with the Spirit in this respect was acknowledged throughout the Middle Ages and after. In return for his favour Dante promises to crown himself with a wreath from the Apollonian tree, the laurel.[6] In this same context it may also be recalled that he attributes his genius to one of the spiritual archetypes which lies on his own particular path of ascent[7] towards the Ultimate, and which is the constellation of celestial lights that is symbolized in the zodiac of our terrestrial firmament by Gemini, in whose sign the sun rose at his birth; and as he passes through this archetypal splendour in the Eighth Heaven on his way to the Empyrean, he invokes its aid for what lies ahead of him.

The hierarchy of the archetypes of art begins with the poetry and the music and the analogous visual blessings which are experienced in Paradise, and it is they which are 'the language of the Gods' in the literal sense. Within this same world of the Spirit, notwithstanding their geographical existence, we must situate Helicon and Parnassus, for a mountain is always symbolic of transcendence.[8]

The higher the domain, the more subject it is to the demands of the Absolute. From the pressure of the Divine Oneness results closely woven unity. Thus, as regards the archetypes, not only is each a synthesis in itself, but it may be said to escape, in relation to the others, the limitative separations to which their various symbols are subject; and for us, who are symbols here in this world of *seeing through a glass darkly* (I. Cor. XIII:12), it means that our own spiritual persons benefit from this escape, whence the promises made to us, in sacred texts, of the unprecedented intensity of Paradisal relationships—not only those between each other, but also between us and the celestial realities which radiate earthly blessings such as virgin nature and the arts. The nostalgias which result on earth from the formal barrier between marveling subject and marvelous object may be said to spring from the 'remembrance'—in the Platonic sense—that those barriers are due to be transcended in the supraformal Hereafter. It is one of the functions of sacred art to arouse such 'remembrance'.

What has just been said in connection with unity must not be taken to imply that differences lose any of their distinctness in Heaven since, on the contrary, owing to the pressure of the Divine Onliness—the Great Solitude as it is termed in Taoism—transcendence brings out the uniqueness of each different reflection of the One-and-Only. That particular impact, for example, which nothing but music has power to make upon the soul cannot fail to be more sharply and more eloquently irreplaceable in the next life than in this; and an analogous remark could be made about poetry and the visual arts.

The celestial archetype of music is often termed 'the music of the spheres'. Shakespeare refers to it symbolically[9] in the lines:

Look how the floor of heaven
Is thick inlaid with patines of bright gold:
There's not the smallest orb which thou behold'st
But in his motion like an angel sings.

He adds, with reference to the obstruction caused by the Fall:

Such harmony is in immortal souls
But whilst this muddy vesture of decay
Doth grossly close it in we cannot hear it.[10]

The obstruction in question cannot in fact be disassociated from the soul's investiture in a clay-derived body which, though once immortal like itself, was doomed by the Fall to decay and ultimately to die, and which meantime intrudes something of its mortal grossness into the psychic substance where, until death it is inextricably interwoven with the senses.

The 'music of the spheres' is the transcendent rhythm and melody to which the soul of unfallen man had access, and which may therefore once again become accessible insofar as the effects of the Fall have been overcome by spiritual effort,[11] or insofar as they may have been providentially mitigated in a soul which is something of a throwback to remote and more 'open' generations. The art of music presupposes some such access,[12] for its primal purpose is to give us a foretaste of that which now 'we cannot hear'; and its power to stir us to the depths of our being depends on the fidelity with which it echoes the transcendent harmony that underlies our nature. But what is true of music is equally true of the other arts: they all imply a presentiment, in their artists, of the analogous celestial harmonies from which painting, sculpture, architecture and poetry are derived, an openness which anticipates in a sense the disencumbrance that will be realized at death from 'this muddy vesture of decay'.

What has been said so far points to the conclusion that to speak 'the language of the Gods' the artist has need of a twofold help from Heaven. All art worthy of the name is a reminder, in one way or another, that to be true to ourselves we must transcend our human nature. The traditional painter thus depicts the face of man with human features subtly but distinctly transfigured; and in a parallel way, at the hands of the traditional architect, stones are seen to lose their heaviness, and to become vibrant with the Spirit.

The Heaven-born tradition to which the artists belong will teach them the necessary canons and offer them the technical means through which they may set about achieving such transformation. But that aid, celestial in origin, then passed down horizontally from generation to generation together with the wisdom of accumulated experience, will not be enough to produce a result of first magnitude. For a work of art which can be said have 'fallen from Heaven' there must clearly be some direct vertical intervention from above. Otherwise expressed, for *the kingdom of God is within you* (Luke XVII:21), the artist has need of his higher nature, and that is why it has always been said that man is not the artist of sacred art. He offers his theme to Heaven—to the Divine Muse—with the prayer, explicit or implicit: 'Express this for me'. The case of *The Divine Comedy* has already been mentioned. In Homer's *Odyssey* the prayer is also explicit: 'Tell me, O Muse, of the man of many devices…' It is likewise explicit in Virgil's *Aeneid*, not to speak of a multitude of other examples; and the meaning of all such prayers could be glossed in keeping with the context of this book: 'Make my poetry—or music or painting or architecture or sculpture—a clear echo or reflection of its archetype', or simply: 'Make it symbolic in the fullest sense'.

## CHAPTER SEVEN

# The Quranic Symbolism of Water

In the Qur'ān the ideas of Mercy and water—in particular rain—are in a sense inseparable. With them must be included the idea of Revelation (*tanzīl*), which means literally 'a sending down'. The Revelation and the rain are both 'sent down' by the All-Merciful, and both are described throughout the Qur'ān as 'Mercy', and both are spoken of as 'life-giving'. So close is the connection of ideas that rain might even be said to be an integral part of the Revelation which it prolongs,[1] as it were, in order that by penetrating the material world the Divine Mercy may reach the uttermost confines of creation; and to perform the rite of ablution is to identify oneself, in the world of matter, with this wave of Mercy, and to return with it as it ebbs back towards the Principle, for purification is a return to our origins. Nor is Islam—literally 'submission'—other than non-resistance to the pull of the current of this ebbing wave.

The Origin and end of this wave lie in the Treasuries (*khazā'in*) of the water which are *with Us* (XV:21). *The Treasuries of Mercy* are also spoken of in just the same terms; and it is clear that these Treasuries are no less than the Supreme Source of Mercy Himself, *ar-Raḥmān*, the Infinitely Good. The Qur'ān also speaks of its own Archetype, *the Mother of the Book*, which is the Divine Omniscience, nor can this Treasury be set apart from those of Mercy, for it likewise belongs to *ar-Raḥmān*, who is the

60

Source of the Book: *The Infinitely Good taught the Qur'ān* (LV:1). We have already seen the connection between mercy and comprehension;[2] and the Treasuries of Water comprise both these aspects of *ar-Raḥmān*, for water is a symbol of Knowledge as well as of Mercy. Al-Ghazālī remarks, with regard to the verse *He sendeth down water from heaven, so that valleys are in flood with it, each according to its capacity* (XIII:17). 'The commentaries tell us that the water is Gnosis and that the valleys are Hearts'.[3]

The differentiation here is in the varying capacities of the valleys, not in the water itself, which has come directly from above and has yet to undergo the influences of soil or stone or mineral. But water which comes up from the earth is in fact differentiated, so that it symbolizes different aspects of knowledge as in the following verse: *And when Moses asked for water for his people, and We said: 'Strike with thy staff the rock', and there gushed forth from it twelve springs, everyone knew his drinking place* (II:60). The differentiation here is not only in the drinkers but also in what they drink; and the last five words are quoted throughout Islamic literature to refer beyond their literal meaning, to the fact that everyone who 'drinks' from the Qur'ān is aware of the particular standpoint that has been providentially allotted to him whether it be that of ritual law, for example, dogmatic theology, or mysticism. Nor is it out of line with the literal meaning, if one remembers that in ancient Israel, each of the twelve tribes had its own particular function.

When the Qur'ān tells us that at the Creation *His Throne was upon the water* (XI:7), it affirms implicitly two waters, one above the Throne and one beneath it, since the Tenant of the Throne is *ar-Raḥmān* with Whom are the Treasuries of Water, or rather Who constitutes Himself these Treasuries. From this duality, the Waters of the Unmanifest

61

and the waters of Manifestation,[4] is the prototype of the duality, within creation, of the *two seas* which are so often mentioned in the Qur'ān.[5] These two seas *one sweet and fresh, the other salt and bitter* (XXV:53) are respectively Heaven and earth which were originally *one piece* (XXI:30). Parallel to this and in a sense based on it, is the Sufi symbolism of ice, for salt water and ice, both representing the untranscendent, are both 'gross' albeit in different ways, when compared with fresh water. It is true that the ocean, as the vastest thing in the whole terrestrial globe, has an altogether transcendent significance. When the Qur'ān says: *If the sea were ink for the Words of my Lord, the sea would be used up before the Words of the Lord were used up* (XVIII:109) it is saying that the symbol is not to be compared with That which symbolizes, namely *the Mother of the Book*, the Sea which is in fact vast enough to contain the Words of God. None the less, by choosing the material seas rather than any other earthly thing for this demonstration, the Qur'ān affirms that they are, for the Infinitude of the Divine Wisdom, the symbol of symbols; but they have this symbolism in virtue of their size, apart from and as it were despite their saltness, for salt water as such is always transcended by fresh water.

The significance of a symbol varies according to whether it is considered as an independent entity or in relation to some other symbol. In relation to wine, water—even fresh water—may represent the untranscendent or the less transcendent, as for example when the Qur'ān mentions that in Paradise the elect are given wine to drink whereas the generality of the faithful drink from fountains of water. This relationship between wine and water is analogous to the relationship between the sun and the moon, for wine is in a sense 'liquid fire' or 'liquid light': but fire and water, inasmuch as both are elements, are on the same plane, and it is possible to consider wine and water as equal complements. Thus in another description of Paradise, the Qur'ān mentions *rivers of water and rivers of wine* without specifying any difference of level. Here it may be said that wine, being 'warm', has the 'subjective' significance of Gnosis in relation to the cold objectivity of water which represents Truth, the Object of Gnosis. But when considered by itself, water has a total significance which transcends the distinction between subject and object, or which includes both subject and object, for inasmuch as it can be drunk, water is a symbol of Truth 'subjectivized', that is, Gnosis; and water can indeed claim to be 'the drink of drinks'. In any case, whatever the drink, water is always its basis.

The following passage, the first part of which has already been quoted in connection with Gnosis, is particularly important for its illustration of the difference between the true and the false, or reality and illusion: *He sendeth down water from heaven so that valleys are in flood with it, each according to its capacity, and the flood beareth swelling foam... thus God coineth the symbols of reality and illusion. Then as for the foam, it goeth as scum upon the banks, and as for what profiteth men, it remaineth in the earth.* In the light of this imagery of the scum which remains visible and the water which disappears we may interpret the verse: *They know only an outward appearance of this lower life* (XXX:7). The *outward appearance* is 'the scum of illusion', whereas what escapes us in this world is the hidden 'water of reality'. We see here the significance of the fountain which holds such an important place in Quranic symbolism. The bursting forth of a spring, that is, the reappearance of heaven-sent water that has become hidden signifies the sudden unveiling of a reality which transcends 'outward appearances', and the drinking of which is Gnosis. But in addition to this objective-subjective symbolism, the fountain has also the purely subjective significance of the sudden opening of an eye, which is implicit in the word '*ayn* which means both 'fountain' and 'eye'. This subjective symbolism is in a sense the more important, because the reason why men see only 'the scum of illusion' is that *their hearts are hardened*, or in other words that 'the eye of the Heart' is closed, *for verily it is not the sight that is blind but the hearts that are blind* (XXII:47); and in one highly suggestive passage the Qur'ān compels us to envisage the possibility of a fountain springing from the Heart: *Then even after that your hearts grew hard so that they were like rocks, or even harder, for verily there are rocks from which rivers gush forth, and there are rocks which split asunder so that water floweth from them* (II:74).

The presence between the two seas of *a barrier beyond which they pass not*, means that the waters of this world are unable to overflow into the next, and that the upper waters refrain from utterly overwhelming the lower waters and allow them to exist as a seemingly separate domain without undue interference from above, at any rate *for a while*—to use the Quranic phrase which is so often repeated to denote the impermanence of this world and everything in it. 'Undue' is a necessary reservation, because the upper waters by their very nature cannot altogether be kept out, any more than water—to revert to the Sufi symbolism—can be kept out of ice. The upper waters, being the original substance to all creation, not only surround but also penetrate this world as its secret reality to which it will eventually return. Thus although the rain, symbolizing this penetration, is only sent down *in due measure*, it is none the less a herald or portent of *the Hour*,[6] that is, the Last Day, when the barrier will be removed and the upper waters will flood this world, transforming its nature and causing the resurrection of the dead, for they are the Waters of Life.

Until then, any presence of life in this world means that a drop of these waters has passed the barrier, but this possibility is limited. *Verily this lower life is but as water which We have sent down from the sky* (X:24). Life is altogether transcendent in relation to this world, where it exists merely as a fleeting loan, ready to 'evaporate' back whence it came as water evaporates back to the sky. Life is a passing trespass of the Beyond on the domain of the herebelow, a brief penetration of soul and body by the Spirit;[7] but the Spirit is not 'at home' in this world—hence the extreme precariousness of life[8]—whereas it is indeed at home in the Beyond: *Verily the Abode of the Hereafter, that, that is Life, did they but know* (XXIX:64).

If it be asked how this symbolism can be reconciled with the earth-depopulating Flood, it must be remembered that although rainfall set the Flood in motion, the actual cataclysm is represented in the Qur'ān as a stormy sea. One of Noah's sons who was drowned is said to have been swept away by a wave, and agitated water is a symbol of vanity and illusion, the waves being images of accident and vicissitude, which are 'unreal'[9] in relation to the water itself whose true nature they are powerless to affect. It is significant that in the Verse of Darkness (XXIV:40) which follows close on the better known Verse of Light, the works of the infidels, having just been likened in their vanity to *a mirage in the desert which the thirsty man reckoneth to be water*, are then immediately likened to what is indeed water but has become 'by accident' so remote from its true nature as to be comparable to a mirage, namely a dark storm-tossed sea. This passage may even be taken as an inexplicit description of the Flood. In any case, there is no doubt that the waves of the flood and the waves of the Red Sea which crashed down upon the pursuers of the children of Israel are a just 'payment in kind' for the passionate perversity of Noah's contemporaries, and of Pharaoh and his ministers. On the other hand, as regards what set the Flood in motion, the symbolism of rain is here tempered and conditioned by the number forty which signifies death[10] or a change of state. Thus the purifying aspect of water may be said to take precedence here over its life-giving aspect. The earth was to be purified for a new state just as the children of Israel were to be purified by the forty years wandering in the desert. We may compare also the purification of Lent. The waters of the Flood were an inseparable part of the Revelation made to Noah of a new religion, symbolized by the Ark, and as such they were waters of Mercy. But any manifestation of Mercy is bound to be terrible for those who refuse it, for it serves to gauge the extreme hardness of their hearts, while for those whose hearts are not hardened the Transcendent is always awe-inspiring, and this aspect of Mercy is expressed by the thunder which so often precedes the rain. *He it is who showeth you the lightning, a fear and a longing, and raiseth the heavy clouds. And the thunder extolleth and praiseth Him, as do the angels for awe of Him* (XIII:12-13).

The awe-inspiring and mysterious transcendence of the upper waters, as also their life-giving aspect, is stressed in the strange and elliptical story of Moses and al-Khiḍr (XVIII:60-82). Moses says to Joshua: *I will not cease until I reach the meeting place of the two seas.* They start out as for a long journey, but they stop for rest on a rock which is, unknown to them, the barrier that separates the two seas. Joshua sets down for a moment the provisions he has brought, which consists of a dried fish; and whether because of the extreme nearness of the Waters of Life, or because a drop of these waters actually falls on the fish, it suddenly comes to life, slips from the rock, and swims away in the sea. Moses does not notice this; and the attention of Joshua who does notice it, is immediately distracted by Satan, so that he does not even mention it to Moses, and they set off once more. At length Moses, exhausted by the journey, suggests that they stop to eat. Joshua remembers that their food has gone, and tells Moses about the miracle of the fish, and Moses understands that the rock must have been *the meeting place of the two seas*, and they retrace their steps. When they regain the rock they find there *one of our slaves unto whom We had given mercy from Our Mercy and knowledge from Our Knowledge.* This person is not named, but the commentaries tell us that it is al-Khiḍr, the immortal Prince of the Solitary Ones (*al-afrād*).[11] The symbolism of this meeting with Moses is parallel to the symbolism of the meeting of the two seas. The salt sea of this world represents, like Moses, exoteric knowledge,[12] whereas the Waters of Life are personified by al-Khiḍr. *Moses said unto him: May I follow thee that from what thou hast been taught thou mayst teach me right guidance. He said: Verily thou canst not be patient with me, for how shouldst thou be patient in respect of that which is beyond the compass of thine experience? He said: God willing, thou shalt find me patient, nor will I gainsay thee in aught. He said: Then if thou go with me, question me of naught until of myself I mention it to thee.*

They set out together, and al-Khiḍr performs three acts of mercy in disguise, but Moses, seeing only the 'scandalous' outside of these acts, is too outraged not to expostulate each time, and the third time al-Khiḍr refuses to let him accompany him any further; but he explains, before they part company, the true nature of his actions. To consider this passage in any detail would be beyond the scope of our subject; but it has at least given us a glimpse of the deviousness of the exoteric path and the extreme nearness of the Waters of Life. For we are already, if only we knew it, at the meeting place of the two seas—witness the miracle of life which is always with us, both in us and about us, but which the powers of illusion persuade us to take entirely for granted.

In setting before us this strange example of inadvertence and forgetfulness in respect of the marvelous incident of the fish, the Qur'ān lays bare the general obtuseness of man's attitude towards Life. There is only One Life, that of the Living, in varying degrees of radiation, with a mere difference of intensity between the elixir strong enough to quicken a dried fish and the less strong elixir which suffices to enable the living to continue to eke out *for a while* their precarious earthly existence. It is thus grossly disproportionate to marvel at the one and to remain unmoved by the other. There can be no true wisdom which does not include the enlightenment of seeing life as the miracle that it is, a supernatural interference which cannot be claimed by nature as a purely natural phenomenon. The Shaykh al-'Alawī tells us that the Divine mystery and miracle of life eludes us because of its extreme transcendence. It is with us, and yet at the same time it is utterly beyond us.[13] The spiritual path is in one sense not so much a journey as a gradual attunement of the soul to the presence of the Spirit, a gradual reconciliation between the natural and the supernatural, between the lower waters and the upper waters, between mind and intellect, between Moses and al-Khiḍr.

In conclusion let us consider another relevant passage, which is from the story of Solomon and the Queen of Sheba (XXVII:20-24). Solomon sends for the Queen in order to convert her to the true religion, and while she and her retinue are on their way he says to his surrounding assembly of men and of jinn: *Which of you will bring me her throne before they come unto me in surrender?* The throne is immediately set before him, and he gives instructions for it to be disguised:

> *Disguise her throne for her; we shall see if she is on the right path, or if she is of those who are not rightly guided. And when she came it was said unto her: Is thy throne like unto this? She said: It is as if it were it. And (Solomon reflected) we had been given the knowledge before her and had surrendered unto God; and she was barred from it by what she was wont to worship apart from God. Verily she was from a disbelieving people. She was told: Enter the courtyard; and when she saw it she reckoned it to be a pool of water and bared her legs. He said: It is a courtyard made smooth with glass. She said: O my Lord, verily I have done wrong unto my soul, and I surrender with Solomon unto God, the Lord of the Worlds.*

The gist of what this exceedingly elliptical narration tells us is that Solomon puts Bilqīs—for so the queen is named—to two tests. She fails in both, but her failure dissolves altogether her resistance to the truth. This in itself would require no comment. It is true that the mistakes in question are, on the surface, totally innocent. Moreover, as regards the throne, she appears to see at least partially through the disguise, since otherwise her answer would have been simply no. None the less it is easily imaginable that the consciousness of being mistaken might well have a profound effect upon the soul, out of all proportion to the nature of the error. But the apparent simplicity of the facts is belied by the gravity of the Qur'ān's comments on them, and the depth of the conclusions that are drawn. We are obliged to suspect that it is not merely a question of error as such, but that the particular nature of the error is all important. In both cases it is a question of failure to penetrate through a disguise. What Solomon says about his purpose in disguising the throne could be glossed: We shall see if she penetrates to the truth of things or if she is one of those who stop short at the 'scum' of illusion. This gloss could be applied also to the other disguise, that of the courtyard. The 'scum' in this case is the illusion that water is present when in fact it is absent. But what is the knowledge which Solomon was given *before her* and of which the condition is that he had *surrendered unto God*? It could not simply be what the words literally suggest, his knowledge that the throne was in fact that of Sheba, and that the courtyard was in fact paved with glass. Such knowledge was no more credit to him than the lack of it was a discredit to her. But we are given a key in the reason why *she was barred from it*, namely her worship of false gods. It was because she took illusion to be reality that she had taken reality to be illusion, that is, she had taken identity to be a mere deceptive likeness. Having demonstrated this last error—for although the Qur'ān does not say so we must assume that Solomon tells her that the throne is in fact hers and that what she had thought to be no more than a vague resemblance is indeed identity—he proceeds to demonstrate the opposite error which is its cause, that is, her worship of false gods, her imagining divinity to be present when in fact it was absent. Here lies undoubtedly what might be called the allegorical meaning of the above-quoted verses. We must remember that when this passage was revealed, the Prophet was undergoing great difficulties for the very reason that the chief men of Mecca were blinded to the presence of truth in his message by their erroneous belief that the truth was present elsewhere, in their own worship of false gods. There are many other passages in the Qur'ān which likewise recount a historical incident which is, in one way or another, analogous to the situation in early seventh century Arabia. Solomon here stands for the Prophet, and Bilqīs sums up in herself the erring leaders of the clans of Quraysh who would not surrender to the One True God because of their involvement with a plurality of false gods. But this allegorical admonition to the chieftains of Mecca and the example of repentance which it holds out to them leaves room for a deeper interpretation that throws light on some of the details which the allegory does not account for.

The Supreme Throne is below its Tenant, but by inverse analogy every earthly throne may be said to transcend the king who sits on it, as is to be seen figured in the Seal of Solomon, if we take the apex of a triangle to be the tenant and its base the throne. Significant of the throne's transcendence is its oneness and its permanence: kings come and go, but their throne remains, ideally, forever unchanged. The question of the throne of Sheba is not that part of the Quranic narrative which is directly relevant to our theme, but it cannot be set on one side, and it serves to bring out a point of general importance, namely that a symbol which represents the transcendent may be said to open out virtually onto the Absolute Transcendent.[14] The higher of *the two seas* is strictly speaking no more than the uppermost part of the created universe; but these Waters of Life, seen from below, are merged with the Treasuries of Water, that is, with the Infinite Beatitude. Now since there is a certain analogy between the pairs Heaven-earth (*the two seas*) and throne-king, the throne may be said to signify not merely the mandate of Heaven but also the Source of that mandate, the Divine King, and thus ultimately the Supreme Self.

71

In considering Solomon's first test it must not be forgotten that Bilqīs is a queen. Her first lapse has thus to be defined, in all accuracy, as that of a queen failing to recognize her own throne, and seen in this light it takes on a more serious aspect. Moreover, like the lapses of Moses and Joshua with regard to the miracle of the quickening of the dried fish, the incident of the throne has a general application, for every man is by definition king of the earth and thereby the possessor of a throne which is his mandate from Heaven. Even in later times men are still conscious of being kings inasmuch as they have powers of intelligence and of will which incomparably surpass those of other creatures; but the majority are more or less in a state of vagueness and uncertainty about their throne, and more or less forgetful that although it, that is, the mandate, is always veiled from them or 'disguised', it is always one and the same. In other words, they are no longer kings except by virtuality; in actuality they are usurpers, since veritable kingship implies an as it were organic connection between king and throne. For the perfect king that mandate, not his human subjectivity, is his true ego, one with the Divine Self. The failure to recognize the throne is thus a violation of the Gnostic precept *Know Thyself*, whereas fulfillment of this principle is *the knowledge* which Solomon *had been given*, and of which the condition is surrender (*islām*) in its highest sense, that is, effacement of the human ego before the Supreme Subject.

The precise words with which Bilqīs answers the question that is put to her are subtly significant in this respect—subtly because there is here a disguise which is in a sense analogous to that of the throne. It is permissible to say for example, that in such a sentence as 'when asked the colour of snow, the blind man said it was black', the word 'white' is disguisedly present, because it is forced into the mind.

So also when the queen is asked, *Is thy throne like this*? And when she wrongly answers: *It is as if it were it*, the right answer is forced into our minds, namely 'it is it'; and these words, *huwa huwa* (literally 'he is he', for *'arsh*, throne, is masculine) constitute the Arabic formula for expressing identity and above all, liturgically,[15] the Supreme Identity.

As Solomon's second test which serves to demonstrate why she could not recognize her throne, the meaning remains much the same as in the allegorical interpretation. There, however, what seems to be present but is in fact absent is Truth as Object, whereas here it is rather a question of Truth in the sense of Subjective Reality. In either case we are reminded of the already quoted verse which likens the works of the disbelievers to *a mirage in the desert which the thirsty man accounteth to be water*; and it will be understood from this and the other examples given of the symbolism of water why Solomon's strategy is so powerfully successful: when she lifts up her robes to avoid wetting them and steps onto the glass pavement of the court, the sudden contact of her foot with the opposite of what it had expected is a directly sensed experience of error, enough in itself to produce a profound 'alchemical' effect upon the soul; but this effect is aggravated beyond all measure by her consciousness that the error is, precisely, about water. Thus her whole outlook, already shaken by her first mistake, is transformed in a moment from heresy to orthodoxy by the shock of discovering 'water' to be absent where she had believed it to be present; and in her saying *I surrender with Solomon*, these last two words are an indication that her surrender is to be understood in the same highest sense as his surrender, namely the effacement of the self before the Self, which is the condition of his Gnosis.

## CHAPTER EIGHT

# The Symbolism of the Luminaries in Old Lithuanian Songs

Lithuanian is the oldest, that is, the most archaic in form, of all living Indo-European languages. It still retains a complexity comparable to that of Sanskrit[1] and classical Greek. Various historical and geographical reasons are given by scholars for this 'lack of development'—so called out of deference to progressism and evolutionism—but there can be little doubt that the direct reason why the language has been so remarkably preserved from decay is the presence, until very recent times, of a deep-rooted oral tradition powerful and vital enough to fulfil many of the functions of literature. We are accustomed to distinguishing between living and dead languages, but in the domain of living languages a further distinction could be made between those that possess a written literature and those that rely entirely on oral tradition, for there is no doubt that 'the letter kills' and that among people who are almost wholly illiterate, language can possess a vitality—and in consequence a relative immunity from degeneration—that for us is almost unimaginable. This question has been treated elsewhere;[2] the question now to be considered is not a linguistic one but it is not altogether unconnected with language, for the songs that are our theme were handed down from a remote past by that oral tradition that has helped to keep Lithuanian so intact.

Since these songs form part of what is often called Lithuanian folklore, let us quote what René Guénon says about folklore in general:

> The very conception of *folklore*, in the generally accepted sense of the term, is based on an idea that is radically false, the idea that there are 'popular creations' spontaneously produced by the mass of people; and one sees at once the close connection between this way of thinking and 'democratic' prejudices. As has been very rightly said, 'the profound interest of all so-called popular traditions lies in the fact that they are not popular in origin',[3] and we will add that where, as is nearly always the case, there is a question of elements that are traditional in the true sense of the word, however deformed, diminished, and fragmentary they may be sometimes, and of things that have a real symbolic value, their origin is not even human, let alone popular. What may be popular is solely the fact of 'survival', when these elements belong to vanished traditional forms, and in this respect 'folklore' takes on a meaning rather close to that of 'paganism', if we consider only the etymology of the word 'pagan' and not its 'polemical' use as a term of reproach. The people preserve, without understanding them, the relics of former traditions which even go back sometimes to a past too remote to be dated, so that it has to be relegated to the obscure domain of the 'prehistoric'; they thereby fulfill the function of a more or less subconscious collective memory, the contents of which have clearly come from elsewhere.[4] What may seem most surprising is that on the closest scrutiny the things so preserved are found to contain above all, under a more or less veiled form, abundant information of an esoteric order, which is, in its essence, precisely what is

least popular, and this fact suggests in itself an explanation, which may be summed up as follows: When a traditional form is on the point of becoming extinct, its last representative may well deliberately entrust to this aforesaid collective memory the things that would otherwise be lost beyond recall; that is in point of fact the sole means of saving what can in a certain measure be saved. At the same time, the lack of understanding that is one of the natural characteristics of the masses is a sure enough guarantee that what was esoteric will be none the less undivulged, remaining merely as a sort of witness of the past for such as, in later times, shall be capable of understanding it.[5]

The four songs that follow illustrate every point that is made in the above quotation. As far as one knows, they were handed down entirely by word of mouth until the eighteenth century, and in more recent times[6] children used to learn them by heart at school. As to their deeper meaning, the veil is in many places a thin one, and many if not all the comments made in this article will seem superfluous to the reader who has knowledge of symbolism. In any case, it is preferable not to break up the text with comments, but to let each song be read uninterrupted as a poem, for they certainly have their rights in this respect. Would it be an exaggeration to say that the fourth and last of those given here is one of the greatest lyrics in the world? And through it, do we not breathe something of the fresh air of a remote antiquity?

The translations given here are taken from a little volume entitled *Old Lithuanian Songs*[7] which is an anthology of forty-seven songs, selected and translated into English by Adrian Paterson. Let us quote what he says of them: 'I have tried as far as possible to render the grace of cadence of the originals, and for this reason I have avoided regular rhymes, which would have given an effect too hard and glib; instead I have done my best to reproduce something of the Lithuanian assonance.'

> Moon took to be his bride
> Sun in the first spring tide.
>
> When Sun woke up at dawn,
> Moon from her side was gone.
>
> Moon, as alone he roved,
> Morn's Star beheld and loved.
>
> Then Thunder, wroth, with His blade
> cleft him in two and said:
>
> Why didst abandon Sun?
> Why, Morn's Star's minion,
> by night didst rove alone?

The language of symbolism is universal, and the sun, whether it be feminine as here and in the Germanic tradition, or masculine as in the Hindu and Greek traditions, always has a spiritual or celestial significance in relation to the moon which, in a positive sense, stands for human perfection. In Christian iconography the cross is often represented with the sun on its right and the moon on its left because Christ, the second Adam, unites in himself two natures, heavenly and earthly; and with the same symbolism the creation of the first Adam, also possessed of two natures, is represented in this song by the marriage of the sun and the moon in the first spring.

The sun, as Spirit, is the daughter of God (*Dievo dukryte*[8] ). God Himself is Perkūnas,[9] literally 'Thunder'; and according to the discourse that Plato, in his *Symposium*, puts into the mouth of Aristophanes, primordial men were of a twofold nature until Zeus, who like Perkūnas has thunder for his chief attribute, cut them in two. But the doctrine of the song is more complete than that of the discourse, for it tells of a double scission: First and 'vertically' there is the separation of sun and moon, that is, Spirit and soul; then as a result of man's loss of connection with his higher possibilities, there is a 'horizontal' scission within the soul itself.

In its highest significance, as we have seen in previous chapters, the moon is the eye of the Heart, primordial man's 'third eye' which alone in the night of the herebelow can see directly the light of the sun, that is, of the Spirit. But the moon is none the less the entirely passive receptacle of solar splendour which it can only refract, with no power in itself to give anything other than this indirect light which corresponds to mental intelligence. In these songs the connecting link between soul and Spirit is not mentioned as an eye but as a marriage; the separation of the luminaries means the loss of the eye. Henceforth man is inwardly divided, since he now lacks contact with the transcendent principle that alone can resolve opposites into complements. In other words, he has become subject to the 'Knowledge of Good and Evil'. It is this division within the soul of man that is represented in the song by the cutting of the moon in two. The soul-dividedness of fallen man, as Titus Burckhardt remarks,[10] is, as it were, the starting point of alchemy; 'chemical marriage', that is, the 'marriage of sulphur and quicksilver,' would thus be, in Lithuanian terms, the putting together again of the two halves of the moon, whereas the 'mystical marriage' would be the remarriage of the moon with the sun.[11]

The Morning Star, Ausrine, is in some respects none other than Lucifer, whereas in other respects she is comparable to Eve. In the second song, which needs no comment, the correspondence is to Lucifer:

> Sun, 'tis time you went
> over the firmament,
> Sun, 'tis time to fare
> through the air.
> Sun, 'tis time you counted
> if all the stars are mounted.
>
> Whether I count or no,
> already one will not show
> and that the star most bright
> which rose up with the light
> and retired late at night.

In the following song the Morning Star represents, like Eve, the fallen human race as a whole:

> Morn's Star held a wedding feast.
> Thunder galloped through the gate
> and struck down the green oak tree.
>
> The blood of the green oak tree trickled,
> and stained my apparel,
> and stained my garland.
>
> The Sun's daughter wept,
> and for three years gathered
> withered foliage.
>
> And where, O mother mine,
> shall I wash my apparel,
> where wash away the blood?
>
> O daughter mine so youthful,
> go to the lake there yonder
> where are poured the streams of nine rivers.
>
> And where, O mother mine,
> shall I dry my apparel
> where in the wind shall I dry it?

O daughter mine so youthful,
in yonder garden green
where are flowering nine roses.

And when, O mother mine,
shall I put on my apparel,
put it on in its whiteness?

O daughter mine so youthful,
on that same day of singing
when there shall shine nine suns.

Owing to a difference of symbolism, this song appears on the surface very different from the first, except that the Morning Star's wedding feast clearly recalls the illicit union which, in the other song, likewise provoked the wrath of Perkūnas. But if we consider the relationship between certain symbols, in particular the sun and the tree, we shall find that the theme of the first song is altogether comprised within the song of the Morning Star and the oak, though this last song takes us further, tracing out not only the Fall but also the path of return to the primordial state.

The Tree of Life rises from the centre of the Earthly Paradise connecting earth with Heaven. Man's loss of connection with his higher possibilities is thus, in the language of Genesis, his loss of access to the Tree of Life, and we have seen this same loss symbolized also by the moon's separation from the sun. In our third song the Tree of Life is the oak which in the Lithuanian tradition is the most holy of trees,[12] being especially sacred to Perkūnas.[13] It might at first seem strange that the Thunderer should strike his own tree, but history offers examples of great sanctuaries being destroyed by Heaven in reprisal for human sacrilege, and here also it is in reality against man's connection with the sanctuary that Perkūnas aims his bolt. Ultimately, therefore, this symbolism comes close to that of Genesis, at least in the sense that in both cases man has lost his access to the Tree of Life. But in the song this scission is also represented by the separation of the leaves from the tree. The analogy between the leaves and the human soul (and therefore the 'moon') is clear enough if we remember that when the cross symbolizes the two natures of Christ, the horizontal line denotes his human nature, which is likewise represented by the leaf-bearing branches of the Tree of Life, whose trunk, like the vertical of the cross, stands for his Divine nature. The symbolism of the leaves becomes even clearer when we consider that the Tree of Life is sometimes also called the 'Tree of the World' or the 'Axis of the World',[14] and as such it is occasionally represented with its roots in Heaven[15] and its branches constituting this world or, microcosmically, the human soul.

If the separation of the foliage from the tree corresponds to the separation of the moon from the sun in the first song, the subsequent scattering of the foliage corresponds to the cleaving of the moon, that is, to the psychic disintegration consequent upon the Fall. The gathering together of this foliage is thus the first phase of the spiritual path, the reintegration of the psychic elements. When all the foliage has been gathered, fallen man turns again to the Spirit. It is as if the moon, now on the way to regaining his primal fullness, were to turn once more to the sun; but the song we are now considering shows us another aspect of the sun. Instead of being man's Celestial Bride, she is here, as in most other Lithuanian songs, his Divine Mother. For if she is the daughter of Perkūnas, she is also, as the Hindus would say, his *Shaktī*, and as such she is the personification of Mercy and the other 'feminine' attributes of the Divinity.

In the purification by the elements, that is, by water, wind, and sun, which now takes place under the direction of the Spirit, the element earth is not mentioned, perhaps because man himself is in a sense earth.

Nine, which is, one might say, the very essence of this song, is a celestial number. There are nine celestial spheres, and nine degrees in the hierarchy of the angels. Moreover, nine corresponds, geometrically, to the circumference of the circle[16] and therefore to the movements of the heavenly bodies and to the visible form of the firmament which is itself the great symbol of Heaven. Nine is therefore also— and here lies the key to this song—the symbol of the Earthly paradise which, as the chief reflection of Heaven upon earth, is always represented as circular; and although in the perspective of later and more 'sedentary' religions the restoration of perfection is the 'squaring of the circle'[17] — the Heavenly Jerusalem, for example, is square—in the earlier and more nomadic perspectives the inverse of the Fall is always a return to the Earthly Paradise. It is therefore not surprising that the number nine should be so much stressed in this song whose theme is, precisely, the recovery of the primordial state which marks the end of the Lesser Mysteries.

In particular, as regards the 'nine suns', here may be here an implicit reference to the restoration of the Tree of Life, for in various traditions there is mention of the shining of a plurality of suns at the end of the cycle, and as Guénon remarks: 'The image of the sun is often connected with that of the tree, as if the sun were the fruit of the Tree of the World'.[18] He mentions, as regards the Hindu doctrine of the end of the cycle, 'the tree whose fruits are twelve suns'.[19] He also draws out attention to the fact that even where there is no specific mention of suns in connection with the Tree of Life, it is often represented as bearing 'solar' fruits: 'The fruits of the Tree of Life are the golden apples of the Garden of the Hesperides; the golden fleece[20] of the Argonauts, which was also placed on a tree and guarded by a serpent or a dragon, is another symbol of the immortality which man has to reconquer'.[21] Finally he mentions that in China one finds also, as a symbol of the completion of the cycle (which in the macrocosm means a new Golden Age and in the microcosm the return to the primordial state), the tree with ten suns; and this brings us back to our song, for as we have already seen, nine and ten are sometimes interchangeable in that both can represent the circle which is itself the figure of the cyclic perfection. Analogously one can say of the Garden of Helicon that it bears the seal of nine or of ten according to whether or not we count, with the nine Muses, Apollo himself who is the centre around which they form the circumference.

The mention of Apollo is, as we shall see, a preparation for the fourth poem:

> Fly little hawk
> near to the lake,
> near that same lake
> where a whirlpool seethes.
>
> Near to that whirlpool
> there's a rue garden.
> In that same garden
> weeps a maiden.
>
> I have no mother
> a dowry to gather,
> I have no father
> to apportion my share.
>
> I have no brother
> to saddle horses,
> I have no sister
> to plait a garland.

Sun, thou mother,
Sun, thou mother,
Sun, thou mother,
gather me a dowry.

Moon, thou father,
Moon, thou father,
Moon, thou father,
apportion my share.

Star, thou sister,
Star, thou sister,
Star, thou sister,
O plait my garland!

Greatwain, thou brother,
Greatwain, thou brother,
Greatwain, thou brother,
O drive me through the meadows!

The hawk, with all the other members of its tribe, above all the eagle, is a solar bird, and as such a symbol of the Spirit. But in particular it may be remembered that whereas the eagle is the bird of Zeus, the hawk is one of the emblems of Apollo, God of inspiration, and in this song the prayer of the maiden is clearly uttered under the inspiration of the hawk, whereas there can be no doubt that the initial imperative addressed to the hawk is a Divine command. In ancient Egypt the equivalent of Apollo was Horus; and it is perhaps not irrelevant to recall here, especially in view of the end of the song, the temple paintings that represent him as the hawk-headed usher of righteous souls into the presence of Osiris.

Rue has been used from time immemorial to ward off evil influences[22] and to purify sanctuaries and habitations in cases of pollution, so that among plants it is one of the outstanding symbols of purity. As such it plays a particularly important part in Lithuanian tradition. The 'rue garden' or 'Garden of Purity', which is difficult of access and 'guarded' by the whirlpool as by a dragon, and which is, moreover, to be the starting point of the maiden's celestial journey, can be none other than the Earthly Paradise. This is also confirmed by the outstanding simplicity, childlikeness, and spiritual poverty of the maiden herself, these being among the terms in which readiness to enter the Kingdom of Heaven is universally described by religion.

The 'garland' mentioned in this and in the previous song (there the 'staining of the garland' means loss of innocence) is the garland of rue which in Lithuania was traditionally part of the insignia of maidenhood and especially of the virgin bride who wore it as a wreath on her wedding day.

The 'dowry' that the 'sun' is to 'gather'[23] is contrasted with the 'share' to be 'apportioned' by the 'moon'. Together they represent the maiden's title to be married, that is, since the marriage is celestial, her eligibility in the eyes of Heaven. As such, the solar treasure can be nothing other than spiritual riches, whereas the lunar 'share' consists of the human virtues that are the reflections of those riches. Being of this world, which is the world of forms, the virtues can be analyzed,[24] differentiated, counted and measured.[25] But the synthesis of the spiritual treasure itself is above form and beyond all reckoning; it is therefore to be 'gathered' and 'stored up' but not 'apportioned'.

This song begins where the previous song ended; its theme is not the Lesser Mysteries but the Greater Mysteries, for the starting point is the state of human perfection. The sun and the moon are once more in their primordial relationship, and the maiden is to set off on her journey wearing the Crown[26] of Purity.

## CHAPTER NINE

# The Seven Deadly Sins in the Light
# of the Symbolism of Number

In the series of single-figure numbers there are two that stand out from the rest as having an essentially Divine significance, namely one and seven; between them, as between alpha and omega, is enacted the whole drama of existence. One is the Creator; two signifies the Spirit,[1] three Heaven[2], four earth, and five man, whose place is as a quintessence at the centre of the four elements, the four points of the compass, and the four seasons of the year, which characterize the earthly state. But man cannot fulfil his function as mediator between Heaven and earth without the transcendent dimension of depth and of height, the vertical axis that passes through the centre of all the degrees of existence and is none other than the Tree of Life. This superhuman dimension is implicit in the central point of quintessence but does not become explicit until the number five is transcended. It is through six that the centre becomes the axis, that the seed becomes the tree, and six is the number of primordial man in the state in which he was created on the sixth day. As universal mediator[3] he measures out, with his six directions, the whole of existence; and beyond six lies that from which existence proceeds and to which it returns. *And God blessed the seventh day, and sanctified it: because that in it He had rested from all his work* (Genesis II:3).

Seven thus signifies repose in the Divine Centre. From that point of view it is the symbol of Absolute Finality and Perfection, appearing in this world as a Divine Seal upon earthly things, as in the number of days of the week, the planets, the sacraments of the church, and many other septenaries, the mention of which would take us too far from our subject. But despite these considerations—or rather because of them—there is, as we shall see, a profound reason why the deadly sins should be seven in number.

In quest of the key to this paradox, the first thing to be remembered is the underlying continuity that exists between Edenic man and the fallen man. At the Fall there was no new creation; virtually man is still a central being. If he were not, there would be no nostalgia in his soul, and the first human perfection, instead of being a norm and an ideal, would be out of reach and as it were alien. But in fact it has never been superseded, whence the doctrine of original sin, which is itself an affirmation of the continuity we are considering. Moreover, a doctrine of sin means a doctrine of atonement: where there is a question, not of irrecoverable loss, but of dormancy and perversion in the soul, there can be reawakening and reintegration. This reversible continuity between primal norm and present fact means that however prone to guilt certain powers of the soul may have become, they were originally innocent. We must remember also in this connection the axiom *corruptio optimi pessima*, the best when corrupted becomes the worst; and if it be asked, 'What is the worst?' we may answer, with regard to the human soul, 'the seven deadly sins'.

At any rate, these sins may be taken as landmarks[4] in the domain of all that is most evil; and the three words *seven deadly sins* in a sense 'add up' to *corruptio optimi pessima*, for the number seven betrays the mysterious presence of an *optimum* in the context of deadly sin, *pessima corruptio*. Here also lies the key to the paradox of the correspondence of the deadly sins to the planets, including the luminaries. Taking them in their traditional order, *superbia* (pride) is related to the Sun, *avaritia* (avarice) to Saturn, *luxuria* (lust) to Venus, *invidia* (envy) to Mercury, *gula* (gluttony) to Jupiter, *ira* (anger) to Mars, and *accidia* (sloth) to the Moon. It would be wrong, however, and even sacrilegious, to invert this manner of expression and to say that the sins are actually represented by these celestial bodies after which, because of their exaltation and luminosity, the very Heavens themselves are named. All that can be said is that the planets are symbols of what is 'best' in the soul; and when these *optima* are corrupted, they still continue to be related to the planets, just as they still continue to bear the seal of seven. In other words, those psychic powers or tendencies that have become the vehicles of deadly powers or tendencies that have become the vehicles of deadly sin were numbered before the Fall, when they held in the soul a place analogous to that of the planets in the firmament. Seven may thus be considered as a mark of identity used by a shepherd that it may continue to show, when a sheep has strayed, the fold to which it rightly belongs and to which it may be brought back.

In considering how it is possible for the 'sheep' to stray so far, let us begin with a fact about one of the sins that is generally known but seldom weighed, and that is not without its implications as regards other sins. A feature that all religions have in common is the concept of anger as an unholy rupture of equilibrium side by side with the concept of holy anger, which is exemplified in Christianity by Christ's driving out the merchants from the Temple and of which the sin itself[5] seems like a parody. Analogously, although the term 'holy avarice' is not used, could it not be said that a miser is a caricature of an ascetic and in rare cases perhaps even potentially an ascetic? The traditional representation of a miser as a half-starved man dressed in rags and carrying a bag of gold would have an altogether different meaning if the gold were to be taken symbolically and not literally. Some misers have been known to endure what would be described, in the case of a Saint, as 'heroic deprivations'. But since *acts are according to intentions*,[6] the two 'poverties' are as remote from each other as hell is from Heaven. None the less—for with God all things are possible—if a great spiritual Master were to take a miser and turn him into a Saint, the avarice, though necessarily rejected, would not have to undergo an absolute rejection;[7] but the word 'turn' is used here advisedly, for the tendency in question would need to be completely reorientated. Thinking along parallel lines, could not something analogous be said of the sin of lust, for example? Passion, if turned away from the world, can give the soul precipitance in the right direction.

In connection with another deadly sin, we may remember the words of the Decalogue: *I the Lord thy God am a jealous God.* Not that 'jealous', as used here, is a synonym of 'envious', but the two may be said to have a common root, namely the refusal to accept that another should have, or be given, something that one feels should come to oneself. Every metaphysician may be said to share in Divine jealousy in as much as he is jealous for God, refusing to let the relative be given that which is due to the Absolute. It is in this discernment, needless to say, and not in its sinful parody, that Mercury comes into his own. Esoterically the jealousy may be transposed once more from objective to subjective mode as a refusal to let the empirical ego usurp the rights of the true self. At a less exalted level we must also remember that the word envy is often used in an altogether blameless sense, as in a sentence such as: 'I envy you your tranquil nature'. To take another example, an Islamic tradition tells us of a man who, having overslept, arrived at the mosque to pray the dawn prayer only to be met on the threshold by men coming out. 'Have you already prayed?' he said to the first of these; and at the affirmative answer he heaved such a sigh of regret that the man he had questioned said, 'Take my prayer, and give me that sigh!' Such spiritual envy has its paradisal archetype in the mutual wonderment of blessed souls at each other's perfection.[8]

As to the worst sin of all, it is significant that in Islam one of the ninety-nine Divine names is 'the Proud'. The Qur'ān uses exactly the same word to glorify God as to condemn Pharaoh; and if God is Proud, then pride must also be an aspect of human perfection, made in His image. We have here a virtue and a vice that bear the same name even though they lie at opposite poles of human possibility; and the truth *corruptio optimi pessima* stands as a bridge across the guilt that appears separate to them. It remains to be seen how it is possible for this bridge to be crossed, both by way of corruption and also, from the other side, by the path of redemption.

As regards corruption, we may take our key from the symbolism of another number traditionally associated with the deadly sins, that is, the number eight,[9] for if seven denotes simply the best, eight in its positive sense[10] denotes the precise degree that this particular best, the best of the corruptibles, holds in the universal hierarchy. In his article on the symbolism of the octagon René Guénon mentions that in sacred architecture an octagonal structure serves as support for a dome, thus marking the transition from the square foundation to the circular summit, that is, from the terrestrial number four to the celestial number nine.[11] In other words, eight denotes the intermediary region between earth and Heaven or, microcosmically, between body and Spirit; and the octagon supporting the dome is particularly relevant here as a symbol of the psychic substance's 'best' part, that part which serves as a vehicle for the spiritual light symbolized by the dome itself. This octagon has in fact a triple symbolism, for not only is it a vehicle of the dome but also, by being immediately adjacent to it, it expresses the nearness to Heaven of the psychic elements in question, and by being almost circular in form it expresses their all but spiritual nature. Moreover, eight is the number of the winds, which signify the inspirations it is the function of these elements to receive. But being of the soul, not of the Spirit, these relative summits are by definition corruptible; and not only has the devil access to them but it is here above all that he intervenes,[12] for he can do no far-reaching harm to a human soul unless he can first pervert one or more of its highest elements, which otherwise, continuing to fulfil their intuitive function, will remain like vigilant sentinels, ever ready to give the alert. It was certainly not to any lower faculties that Satan's original temptation was addressed, but rather to those that constitute man's leanings toward the next world, his hopes of immortality, his longings for the untransitory. This is brought out clearly in the Quranic account of the fall: *Then Satan whispered unto him,*[13] *and said: 'O Adam, shall I show thee the tree of immortality and a kingdom that fadeth not away?* (XX:120). Let us quote also the following comment on this:

All his deception of mankind throughout the ages[14] is summed up in the above verse; he ceaselessly promises to show man the Tree of Immortality, gradually reducing by this means the highest and most central faculties into the outer part of the soul so that he may imprison them there in attachment to the counterfeit objects which he has forged for their perception. It is the presence here of these perverted faculties, either in discontent that they can never find real satisfaction, or finally in a state of atrophy in that they are never put to their proper use, which causes all the disorder and obstruction in the soul of the fallen man.[15]

To take particular examples, it could be said that the sin of gluttony is caused by the erring presence, in the outer or lower part of the soul, that part that is nearest the senses, of a perverted psychic element whose rightful place is at the threshold of Heaven and whose normal function is to represent, for the individual in question, what might be termed the sense of the Infinite. True to its nature, it still looks for infinite satisfaction but it is condemned to do so in the most finite domains. A similar erring presence can be said to lie at the roots of the already mentioned sin of lust.

On the other hand, the static or contractive sins of sloth and avarice can be traced to a perverted sense of Eternity. The one is the attempt to realize eternal peace in a domain that is divinely willed to be in a state of movement and vicissitude. The other is the attempt to keep eternally that which is, by its very nature, ephemeral; it is also the blindness of attributing to 'treasure upon earth' the absolute value that belongs only to treasure in Heaven.

Eternity and Infinity are dimensions of the Absolute, and the perverted sense of the Absolute, either directly or through one or other of these dimensions, may be said to lie at the root of all deadly sin. It is the 'reverberation' of the Absolute, however remotely, that alone can account for the monstrousness of the semi-insane exaggerations in question.

The sin of anger presupposes as much lack of sense of proportion as avarice does, though in an altogether different mode; either could be described as the 'absolute' effect of a relative cause. But avarice is the deification of a material object, whereas anger, like the sins of envy and pride, implies a certain deification of the ego, its endowment with rights that belong only to the Absolute, that is, to the Supreme Self. But at the summit of the soul of the Saint there are necessarily elements of sublime 'thunder and lightning', just as there are necessarily elements that may be said to participate in the divine jealousy inasmuch as they 'begrudge', through their discernment, the attribution of any absolute value to other than the Self. Similarly, having realized the answer to the question 'Who am I?'[16] the Saint cannot fail to participate in the Divine Pride, which will be reflected in the outer part of the soul, not as the sin of pride, but as the virtue of dignity and sometimes even of majesty.

The intuitive part of the psychic substance, the part through which the soul may be said to have the sense of the Absolute, the Infinite, and the Eternal, can be fully operative only if all its elements are in their rightful place. The soul of the Saint is in perfect order and harmony; fallen souls are in a state of disorder that varies incalculably from individual to individual. Needless to say, it is possible that part of the higher substance should remain relatively unfallen. Otherwise there could be no initial other-worldly aspirations, and the individual in question could never become a novice for the spiritual path. But as to those higher elements that are disintegrated and fallen, until they cease to live beneath themselves, that is, until they vacate the places they have usurped on the periphery of the soul, they will continue to cause there perversion or obstruction according to whether they are virulent or dormant.

In connection with the widespread dormancy of psychic elements, it is particularly ironical that the notion of sincerity—or rather the word, for it is scarcely more than that—should loom so large in twentieth-century complacence, for sincerity, which implies an integral vigilance, is just what modern man most lacks. The often heard words 'sincerity is all that matters' express, if duly weighed, a profound truth; but it is nearly always forgotten that sincerity cannot be assessed without reference to what one is sincere about. In other words, the quality of the subjective reaction is inextricably dependent on the quality of the object. To take particular examples, it is really no less than a contradiction in terms to speak of a 'sincere humanist' or a 'sincere communist' if the word 'sincere' is to retain its sense of total commitment. Enthusiasm, everyone now knows, is no guarantee that the subject is sincere. This century, especially in its second half, is witnessing without respite the most violent orgies of enthusiasm, and as often as not the object is so worthless that the 'enthusiast' can be no more than a small fraction of a soul, a fraction that has, perhaps momentarily, declared itself independent of reason, memory, and other faculties. Such cases may not be too dangerous in themselves, but they are alarmingly symptomatic of a widespread psychic disintegration. To revert to the less paroxysmal but much more chronic, and therefore more dangerous enthusiasms of the humanist and the communist, we have only to consider what man is to see that neither humanism nor communism has anything whatsoever to offer to the higher reaches of the human soul.

If such an enthusiasm is none the less able to gain a lifelong grip of any given individual, it can do so only without the assent of his higher psychic elements; and the negative presence of these elements in his soul, whether they be dormant or atrophied, means a virtual inward dividedness which precludes sincerity. It may be objected that in some cases such elements are perverted without being dormant and that the soul can be something of a chaos but none the less 'all there' and therefore sincere; and there can be no doubt, as regards the two enthusiasms in question, that they are able to gain their formidable impetus only by drawing, to a considerable extent, on the soul's latent treasuries of idle and unused spiritual fervour. But such thefts can never be total; perversion is always fragmentary. Fervour is, in its highest sense, no less than the thirst for the Absolute, the Infinite, and the Eternal, and there can be no common measure between the psychic vehicles of this fervour when in their rightful place at the summit of a normal soul, and a mere fraction of them that has been perverted and dangerously bottled up as part of an enthusiasm for some finite and ephemeral object.

Only religious orthodoxy at its fullest—that is, when endowed with the full range of its third dimension of mysticism—is large enough to enlist the whole psychic substance of man and coordinate it into sincerity worthy of the name. The Truth is Indivisible Totality and demands of man that he shall be no less than one undivided whole; and it is a criterion of orthodoxy that it should stake a claim in every element of our being.

But how does mysticism bring about the inverse of *corruptio optimi pessima*, that inverse which is expressed by *the stone which the builders rejected is become the head of the corner* (Mark XXII:10)[17] and also by *joy shall be in Heaven over one sinner that repenteth more than over ninety and nine just persons which need no repentance* (Luke XV:7)?[18] The first phase of the spiritual alchemy of repentance is 'the descent into Hell', so called because it is first necessary to penetrate into the depths of the soul in order to regain consciousness of the 'worst' which by 're-penting' is to become once more the best. But it must be clearly understood that this 'descent' is radically different from any psycho-analytical probing of the subconscious. Modern psycho-analysis is a case of the blind leading the blind; and even when the leader is less blind than the led, it is still merely one soul working on another, without the help of any transcendent power. But in a spiritual path worthy of the name, the guide is the Spirit itself, personi-fied by the Master, and operative in the rites which enable the 'traveller' to advance. Moreover the word 'descent' must not be allowed to mislead us. In Dante's epic, no doubt for reasons of form, the *Inferno* and the *Purgatorio* are distinct. But although he could not represent himself as descending into the infernal abyss at the same time that he was ascending the Mountain of Purgatory, the process of gaining consciousness of guilt and the process of purifi-cation are in fact to a large extent simultaneous; nor could it be otherwise.

What the soul is incapable of doing for itself or for another soul can be achieved by the Spirit, whose pres-ence, vehicled by the rites, demands in response the pres-ence of the soul in its entirety. The perverted psychic ele-ments cannot fail to manifest themselves, but they do so despite themselves, and some of them come in anger, with the infernal powers still attached to them. From this point of view it is truer to say that Hell rises than that the mystic descends; and the result of that rising is a battle[19] with the soul as a battlefield. This corresponds to what in Sufism is called the *Greater Holy War*.[20] Those elements which have become the soul's lowest possibilities must be set free from the powers of darkness and forced to renounce the relativi-ties to which they have become all too absolutely attached. Needless to say *the war against the soul*,[21] that is, against its inward evils, is not easily won. But if the main part of the soul is constant, and continues to wield the invincible weapons given it by the Spirit, the enemy is bound to surrender.

Once emptied of their unworthy contents and disencumbered from the illusions which had stunted and warped them, the reclaimed elements have then to be reminded of their true nature. This phase of love and recall may be said to follow that of fear and renunciation, *for fear of the Lord is the beginning of wisdom*; but here also there is a certain simultaneity, inasmuch as love is an essential factor in the alchemy of purification. Love means consciousness of the bonds of the Absolute, and it is above all this consciousness that has power to loosen the bonds of relativity. The Spirit may be said to address the soul's fallen elements with exactly the same message as that which originally seduced them; but this time the message is true, and a true message is infinitely more powerful than a false one: *O Adam, shall I show thee the Tree of Immortality and a Kingdom that fadeth not away?* The elements concerned, those that were made for nothing but the transcendent, are now merely being asked to conform to their own nature, so that this promise of the transcendent is bound to prove, sooner or later, irresistible—whence the exaltation, by spiritual masters in all ages and all religions, of the virtues of resolution, perseverance, patience and trust.

## CHAPTER TEN

# The Symbolism of the Mosque and the Cathedral in the Light of the Stations of Wisdom

In his *Stations of Wisdom*, in a final chapter which gives its title to the book, Frithjof Schuon defines and expounds six aspects of wisdom which may be said to sum up the whole of spirituality. In other words, they include all that the Will of Heaven demands for man, and therefore they represent the perfection which he possessed primordially at his creation, according to that Will, 'in the image of God'. Man's microcosmic plenitude, in view of the exact analogy between microcosm and macrocosm, corresponds to the full extent of the greater outer world, that is, the six directions of space which are the four points of the compass and the vertical axis of height and depth. Given their fundamental importance, the stations cannot fail to be present more or less explicitly in the doctrine and method of every esoterism no matter what tradition it belongs to. Sacred texts are in fact woven with isolated formulations of these aspects of wisdom, none of which are neglected, and all of which were taken for granted by our ancestors, in varying degrees of consciousness, as being in the nature of things. But the time had come when it was necessary to stress this last point, and to reveal the aspects as an inter-related six-fold totality, namely as the microcosm's 'directions of space', analogous to their counterpart in the macrocosm;

and this we own to Schuon in his *Stations of Wisdom*, and in sections of his other writings.

The universality of this doctrine is clearly demonstrated in *A Treasury of Traditional Wisdom* by Whitall Perry[1] who has divided his monumental work into three books, each of which is subdivided into two parts. The three main divisions correspond to the three *margas* (ways) of Hinduism, action, love and knowledge, as also to the three basic principles of Islamic mysticism, fear, love and knowledge. Each of these divisions has two aspects: the domain of fear-action is that of 'must not' and 'must' or, in Schuon's terms, abstention and accomplishment; love has likewise, in addition to its dynamic intensity, the static aspect of contemplative bliss; and spiritual knowledge is both objective and subjective, being ultimately concerned with the Absolute as Transcendent Truth and Immanent Selfhood. But lest the claim that all spirituality is comprised within these six stations should be thought extravagant, let it be added now—and it will become still clearer in what follows—that each station is a vast synthesis made up of many subsidiary aspects, inextricably linked with one another. It could not be otherwise, for a station is something that has to be adopted: it demands presence on the part of man, his total presence, that is, sincerity; and since man consists of intelligence, will and character,[2] there must be something in every station to enlist each of man's three spiritual faculties—doctrinal or theological elements for the intelligence, methodic elements for the will, and moral elements or virtues for the character.

It follows from what has been said so far that the stations of wisdom might be called dimensions of holiness; and since a work of sacred art in the true sense of the term is as a crystallisation of sainthood which it sets before man as a model, it is bound to reflect these six faces of spirituality. A striking example is to be found in Islamic architecture which is all more or less a prolongation of the mosque. Ecclesiastical architecture has likewise, as we shall see, the same sixfold message; but since the correspondences here are in certain respects more complex and less immediately obvious, let us first consider how the stations, one by one, are reflected in the different elements of the mosque.

*Fear of the Lord is the beginning of wisdom*, and it is to fear that the first two stations are related. They are thus concerned with danger, and they are two because danger confronts man with two possibilities, flight or attack. The Qur'ān expresses the former of these in the words, *there is no refuge from God except in Him* (IX:118). This truth-precept is as it were echoed in the holy Tradition *Lā ilaha illa Llāh*[3] *is My fortress*; *and whoso entereth My fortress is safe from My punishment*. This station's aspect of taking sanctuary is obviously one that the mosque as a whole is qualified to express: but it does so most directly by the door through which refuge is taken, and by the protective walls.

A station is by definition and even by etymology static: but within this framework some of the stations are dynamic. The first is however purely static: to pass through the door and, in doing so, to turn one's back on the outer world need not be reckoned as a movement, for it is relatively instantaneous. What counts here is the safety and its condition of not leaving the sanctuary but remaining faithfully inside it, shut away from temptations in 'an inner separation from the false plenitude of the world. The withdrawal corresponds to the stage of renunciation or detachment, of sobriety, fear of God'.[4] Let us quote also: 'The Divine prototype of the virtue of detachment is Purity, Impassibility, Immortality; this quality, whether we envisage it *in divinis* or in ourselves, or around us, is like crystal, or snow, or the

cold serenity of high mountains'.[5] As Schuon has said elsewhere, this station corresponds to the North, and to the
season of Winter.

It goes without saying that a stone replica of a station,
being incomparably more limited than the station itself,
can only register those aspects which are within the range
of its own particular mode. None the less, if we take as an
example any one of the great mosques which represent the
full flowering of the art in question, who can fail to be
struck by the contrast between the noise and agitation that
is left behind and the peace-giving motionless silence that
is offered by the sanctuary thanks to the massive thickness
of its walls, which in themselves, in their impregnable
steadfastness, serve as a summons to steadfastness of soul
which is one of the basic virtues of this station. To enter
the mosque is also to be immediately and profoundly impressed by its emptiness, both as antidote to 'the false plenitude of the world' and as symbol of the inner void of purity. This, in the heat of Summer, is confirmed from yet
another angle, since to pass through the great portal is to
be met by a wave of coolness which conspires with the
silence and the emptiness to give wings to the initial renunciation, that is, to transform it into the inviolable detachment wherein this station has its fulfillment and
wherein the framework of fear is transcended to retrieve
its primordial aspect of awe.

The second station, also primarily one of fear, is concerned with the positive reaction to danger, namely attack,
and it includes 'the Greater Holy War', while at the same
time it goes beyond it in more than one direction. 'The
symbols of this spiritual station—that of combat, victory,
pure act—are lightning or the sword; it is *in divinis* flash-
ing and invincible Perfection, and in man, holy anger or
holy warfare, but above all the inner act as affirmation of

the Self'.[6] At first thought it may be wondered how a building could possibly represent anything so essentially dynamic as this station, but as we enter the mosque the answer becomes immediately clear and in some cases, that of the great mosque of Córdova for example, overwhelmingly clear, which is as it should be, for it is in the nature of this station to overwhelm. In the domain of the static the pillar is dynamic in virtue of the tenseness of its architectural function. From the standpoint of this mode of fear, 'what has to be actively conquered is natural and habitual passivity towards the world and towards the images and impulsion of the soul; spiritual laziness, inattention, dreaming, all have to be overcome'.[7] The pillar, by its upward thrust, counteracts gravity which corresponds to 'natural and habitual passivity'. Stone is by its nature inert and heavy, but through the hands of the architect it may be inspired with a heavenwards inclination; and since the architect is himself the symbol of the Great Architect of the universe, we are reminded here of the creation of man *in the fairest uprightness* (Qur'ān XCV:4). This rectitude of soul, outwardly prolonged in man's vertical stance, marks him, and him alone, as the mediator between Heaven and earth, a function manifestly symbolized in a building by that which mediates between the roof and the floor.

The context of primordiality is a reminder that this station corresponds, in the annual cycle, to the season of Spring, when the sap rises in the trees, and the earth puts forth new growth after its season of retreat. Analogously it corresponds to the East, where the sun rises victorious over the shadows of night; and the pillar, by its verticality, is an image of waking, uprising, vigilance and alertness. But above all, because of its being in the form of the Arabic letter *alif* and of the numeral one, both of which, in their different ways, express the One Truth,[8] the pillar is a figure of the 'inner act of affirmation'.

In this last respect it must be noted that the pillars are active not only each in itself for the reasons already given, but also collectively in virtue of their reiteration, which is one of their most essential features. But for their multiplicity, the mosque would have no extension in space, just as the affirmation, if not uttered again and again, would have no duration in time. The pillars conquer space for the mosque by their relentless repetition—pillar after pillar after pillar—just as the reiterated *alif*—affirmation after affirmation after affirmation—conquers the flow of life by 'the transmutation of time into instantaneity'.[9] The inward act perpendicularly outrules past-future horizontality by forever reasserting the Eternal Present, which is symbolized by the vertical dimension.

The aim and end of the Greater Holy War is to establish the Greater Holy Peace; analogously, the pillars serve to make the roof rest securely in its pride of place as the Heaven of the mosque. It is to the third station, the passive mode of love, that the roof corresponds, and above all the dome. 'Passive virtue is made up of contemplative contentment...it is the calm of that which is at rest in itself, in its own virtue'.[10] By its circularity the dome relates to the number nine, which is a celestial number, and the circle is moreover the most peaceful of all forms. 'The quality of calm derives from the Divine Peace which is made of Bliss, of Infinite Beauty; beauty everywhere and always has at its root an aspect of calm, existential repose'.[11] Amongst the various features of the building the dome is strikingly a domain of beauty, and it is there that the builders tend to be especially lavish with their ornamentation.

The number three, which is also a celestial number, corresponds to the triangle and therefore to the pyramid which replaces the dome in Moorish architecture. The pyramid is a figure of upward tendency, but having nothing to support, it is altogether without tension. It marks the change from a terrestrial to a celestial centre of gravity, and in doing so it is a reminder that one aspect of this station is 'to repose upwards as a bird reposes in flight'.[12]

The arches are not without tension, but they may be said to anticipate the roof and the dome which they support, and to partake of their symbolism. The rectangular or square base of the building corresponds to the terrestrial number four, whereas all that is curbed is celestial. 'In Masonic initiation the passage "from square to arch" represents in fact a passage "from Earth to Heaven",[13] that is, from the domain of the "Lesser Mysteries" to that of the "Greater Mysteries".... Circular and square forms are also indicated by the compass and the set square which serve to trace them respectively and which together symbolize two complementary principles such as those of which Heaven and Earth are in fact an example'.[14] In this connection, since there has already been mention of the correspondence between a work of sacred art and works of Divine art such as the human microcosm, it is relevant to recall here that in the bodily microcosm its 'heaven', namely the head, is round, whereas the shoulders, which may be said to mark the end of the corporeal frame, are square.

The dome's privilege as a remarkably apt vehicle for ornamentation is shared by the prayer-niche which also corresponds to love, but to its active mode. The dome is static; it rests effortlessly on the structure like a crown of beauty and peace. The primary significance of the prayer-niche is, on the other hand, to give worshippers their orientation: it demands that they turn towards the All-Merciful, and it shows them how to turn. 'Turning towards' means fervour, which is an essential aspect of this fourth station. 'It is the melting of the heart in the heat of the Divine, its opening to Mercy'.[15] Orientation always implies an activity for the sake of a passivity, a turning towards Heaven in order to be attracted by Heaven; and the inviting nature of the niche's roundly recessed hollow is a symbol of this Merciful attraction.

The niche has a dynamic quality not only in virtue of its spiritual magnetism but also because it is the domain of the movements of the ritual prayer which signify a gradual melting until, in the prostration, the body—and with it the soul—finally pours itself out, as it were, in the direction of Mecca. The chief orison which is uttered in the Islamic ritual prayer is *Guide us upon the straight path* (Qur'ān I:6) and the Arabic word for 'straight', *mustaqīm*, suggests not only directness but also vertical ascent. There is however no discrepancy between this and the orientation, which points not simply from place to place on the same level but from periphery to centre. In other words, it interiorises; and interiority places us on the vertical axis. The prostration in or towards the niche is the symbol of an inner vibration of fervour towards the Heart, the centre of the microcosm and, for man, the sole outlet to the Beyond. It should be remembered in this connection that there is not only a certain symbolical equivalence between inwardness, centrality and depth, but also between these and height, for they all imply beyondness or transcendence. The Heart is the gateway to the Spirit, which is hierarchically 'above' the Heart; yet it is nonetheless true to say that access to the Spirit lies 'in the depth' of the Heart. In a parallel way, the sky is the great symbol of God's Kingdom; but *the Kingdom of God is within you*. The equivalences in question spring from the antinomy that the Absolute is both All-Encompasser and Centre from which all radiates.

The stations are complementary to each other in different ways. 'The point of view of fervour or of life is harmoniously opposable to that of detachment or death, just as the point of view of contentment or of peace is opposable without contradiction to that of action or of combat'.[16] In considering this last station, we have already seen how the pillar is an image of 'the inner act of affirmation'; and since the act is rooted in the Divine,[17] it could not be in contradiction with the Divine Peace. The perfect complementarity of the stations of effort and repose is displayed throughout the mosque by the harmonious conjunction of the pillars and the arches. As to the fervent station of turning towards God, its correspondence to the South and to the season of Summer is a feature of its complementarity with the cold station of turning away from the world in steadfast and sober detachment; and as if to express this relationship, the prayer-niche appears in some mosques like a little oasis of life in the desert of the walls. More generally speaking, it is likewise evident that in every mosque the walls are a barrier to the outer world, whereas the niche is an opening to the inner world of the Hereafter.

'The plane of knowledge, which by definition goes beyond the realm of the *ego* as such, comprises a separative mode and a unitive mode, as the very nature of gnosis requires; or, as could also be said, an objective mode and a subjective mode, in the deepest sense of these terms. Knowledge in fact operates either by discrimination or by identification: either, it is "perceiving" or "conceiving", or else it is "being".'[18] Since they go beyond the 'horizontal' human plane which is measured out by the four points of the compass, the two modes of knowledge correspond to

the vertical axis, discrimination to height and identification to depth. As to the discriminative objective mode, this
fifth station of wisdom is symbolized by the minaret of the
mosque. Like the pillar, the minaret is alphabetically an
*alif*, which stands for the Supreme Name, and numerically
the figure one which affirms the Divine Oneness; but, unlike the pillar, having no weight to carry, it is not fraught
with any 'subjective' tension. It remains thus a purely static
and objective affirmation of Truth—objective because its
function is to be a clear object of sight from far and wide,
a symbol of the Distinct, the Evident.[19] Its function is also,
and above all, to be the object of hearing, for it is ritually
the place of the call to prayer. This summons, in which the
words 'come to the prayer' are pronounced only once, consists mainly of affirmations of the Transcendent Oneness
of God (*Lā ilāha illa Llāh*) and of His Transcendent Greatness (*Allāhu akbar*, God is Greatest); and in virtue of its
height, by which it far transcends the rest of the building,
the minaret is itself the very image of Transcendence.
Moreover, it is free from the multiplicity, for even if a
mosque have more than one minaret, only one is needed;
nor is there room on it for more than one muezzin. Its formal symbolism of Oneness is thus confirmed from other
angles.

Within the mosque the pulpit may be considered as an
extension of the minaret, corresponding to the fifth station
both in virtue of its elevation and because it is the domain
of truth. The traditional Islamic sermon is a purely objective formulation of doctrine and of law based on the Qur'ān
and the sayings of the Prophet. The preacher becomes the
mouthpiece of these two sources, his subjectivity being as
it were extinguished, the more so since the pulpit is so
constructed that his face is hidden from most of the con-
gregation. In the perspective of this station 'the subject is

false; the Object alone is true; the subject is individuation, illusion, limitation; the Object—that is to say that which is 'outside of us'—is the Principle, the Absolute'.[20] On the other hand, from the standpoint of the knowledge which unites and identifies, 'the Subject is true and the object is false; the Subject is the Infinite Self, and the object is that which veils It, namely limited or objectified consciousness'.[21] What is then the symbol, in the mosque, of the true Subject? Or in other terms, since the Heart, the centre of the soul, is ultimately, in its depth of depths, the Throne of the Divine Self, what can be considered as the heart of the mosque? There is one main answer to our question, but there are also some subsidiary answers which we will mention first.

The sixth station of wisdom may be said to absorb into itself the other stations, all of which lead up to it, each in its own way. 'In this ultimate knowledge, there is no more discriminating, there is nothing but pure Light; it is identity, not confrontation'.[22] Many of the great mosques have a central courtyard open to the sky, a point of vantage from which it is possible to take in all those symbolic features which have so far been considered. This centre is thus a station of totality; and its openness, being from within, signifies the Infinitude of the Self's inward dimension.

A mosque may also be centered on a sanctuary: in the three holiest mosques of Islam, taking them in order of precedence, the Heart is represented respectively by the Ka'bah, the tomb of the prophet, and the rock of his Night Ascension. By extension from the second of these, many a mosque has been built round the tomb of a Saint. To visit such a shrine is to partake, if only remotely, of the wisdom of all the stations that lies personified and unified there. Again by extension, since to be man is to have a virtual if not an actual holiness, it can be said that the heart of the

108

mosque is the living worshipper himself. Here is in fact the main answer to our question, since every mosque centres round those who worship in it and who are thus the very reason for its existence. We will come back to this point later.

Most of the correspondences so far mentioned between the stations and the various features of the mosque apply no less precisely to the cathedral, which has likewise not only its worshippers but also its doors and protective walls, pillars and arches, pulpit and roof, sometimes a dome,[23] and often a steeple or spire of which the symbolism may be said to coincide, though not in every respect, with that of the minaret. But to say no more than this would be a grave simplification, as will be seen from a brief glance at the main differences between these two forms of temple and what it is, in the two perspectives, which lies at the root of these differences.

In no religion is greater stress laid on orientation than in Islam: the ritual prayer must be prayed in the direction of Mecca wherever in the world the Muslim happens to be. It might therefore seem a paradox at first sight that there is, in the mosque, no architectural 'movement' or 'flow' from door of entry to niche of prayer. But it must be remembered that primarily[24] the niche is not an end in itself; it serves to indicate the direction towards something which is at a certain distance; and though that object, the Ka'bah, is often named 'the House of God', this must not be understood as a localisation of the Divinity. *Wheresoever yet turn, there is the Face of God. Verily God is Vast, All-Knowing* (Qur'ān II:115). This revealed expression of the Divine Omnipresence may be said to dominate Islamic architecture, and to account for the absence, in the mosque, of anything equivalent to the nave of a church.[25] Also dominant in a similar sense is a verse addressed to the Prophet:

*If My slaves ask thee of Me, say I am Near. I answer the prayer of the pray-er when he prayeth* (II:186). Another revealed verse which may be quoted here is *We (God) are nearer to him (man) than his jugular vein* (L:16). All these revelations help to explain why, on entering the mosque, one is immediately confronted by a marked difference between it and the cathedral, namely its emptiness, which is the perfect receptacle for the Divine Omnipresence. The above verses also enlighten us as to why 'Nothing expresses effort in Islamic architecture, there is no tension, nor any antithesis between Heaven and earth'.[26] The following remark is likewise most relevant: 'It is by its immobility that the atmosphere of a mosque is distinguished from all things ephemeral….In this architecture the beyond is not merely a goal, it is lived here and now, in a freedom exempt from all tendencies; there is a repose free from all aspiration'.[27] One can hardly fail to be aware of the conformity between such a setting and the hands of a Muslim in supplication which are held in a position of purely passive receptivity with palms open and upward like those of a beggar hoping to receive alms from the generosity of a passer-by. By contrast, a pair of Christian hands in prayer are an image of upward aspiration, an image which finds its analogue in the ascending tendency of the Gothic cathedral, and above all in the spire. Not that there can be any doubt that the spire, like the minaret, is a monumental affirmation of the Transcendent One-and-Only, constructed to be seen from far off, and also to be 'heard', because even though it does not always house the bells, their sound is inevitably associated with the sight of it. But at the same time, unlike the minaret—and this concerns the aspect of love—the spire may be said to absorb into itself all the upward vibrations which lie beneath it, both human otherworldly leanings and their symbolic counterparts in stone, and to transmit them to Heaven. 'Christian mysticism is closely akin to the perspective of renunciation and purity, as also to that of love and mercy; Christianity thus compensates its aspect of renunciation by the passion of love'.[28] The special affinity which Christianity has with these two stations could not be exclusive of the others. But it enables us to grasp easily why, for example, the spire of a church should stand not only for the fifth station as such but also for this same station as a sublimation of the fourth, that of love in its active mode. We are reminded here of Christ's likening *the Kingdom of Heaven* to the *one pearl of great price*, for the sake of which, in order to buy it, the merchant *went and sold all that he had* (Matt. XIII:45–6). The spire points to the 'one pearl', while expressing, at the same time, total commitment to it.

In contradistinction from the mosque, the cathedral is a deliberate localisation, not of the Absolute, which is what Islam means by *Allāh* and which clearly cannot be localised, but of him whose Divine nature is the Second Person of the Trinity. In other words, it is as a crystallisation in stone of the Saviour; and since one of his symbols is the sun, he being *the light of the world*, his building is orientated in the literal sense of the word, even to the point of being turned as precisely as possible towards where the sun rises at the Equinox. Thus, inasmuch as the Vernal Equinox is never very far from Easter, the feast of the Resurrection, the orientation has a temporal as well as a spatial significance. The crucial form[29] of the edifice as a whole represents the body of the Redeemer: his feet are at the West, his head at the East, his outstretched arms are the North-South transept, and his heart is the altar.[30]

The four points of the compass have already been mentioned as being analogous to the first four stations. But to avoid drawing false analogies, let it be born in mind that in the last paragraph the context is very different. The West-East axis of the cathedral takes great precedence over the North-South axis, whereas in themselves, and therefore as regards their correspondence to the stations, the four points or directions are of equal significance. Admittedly the vertical axis of height and depth, may be considered superior to the two horizontal axes of the compass. But both these have a transcendent aspect in virtue of which they can be reabsorbed into the vertical axis. 'The perspective of metaphysical discernment, of the unique and exclusive Reality, is like a synthesis, but on the plane of the Intellect and in transcendent mode, of the two perspectives of the will, that of detachment and that of action; in an analogous way, the perspective of identity or of the Self, is like a synthesis, but on the plane of unitive knowledge and beyond the human level, of the perspectives of peace and of fervour.'[31] Moreover, each of the first four stations has in itself, as we have seen, a Divine aspect, even to the extent of being rooted in the undifferentiated Oneness of the Essence; and this Oneness, symbolized by the central meeting point of the six directions, not only imposes various combinations but confers a virtual unity on the stations taken together, as well as a virtual totality on each station. All these convergences lend themselves to being reflected in sacred art in addition to the divergences.

An immediately striking example of this is offered us, by both mosque and cathedral, in their symbolizing of the first station. The main portal of the cathedral is at the West whereas that of the mosque is not approached from any specific direction. But neither can be truly entered except by turning one's back on the world, so that both correspond to the first station, that of cold detachment and purity, which itself is symbolized by the North and by the season of Winter. It must be remembered however that 'A sanctuary is like a door opening on the beyond, on the King-dom of God. That being so, the door of the sanctuary must itself recapitulate the nature of the sanctuary as a whole… The architectural form of a church portal[32] constitutes by itself a sort of summary of the sacred building, for it com-bines two elements: the door and the niche'.[33] Impressive examples of the same combination are to be found in dif-ferent styles of mosque architecture; and since here the entire building is as it were included between the door and the prayer-niche, that is, between the entrance and the ulti-mate reason for which the entrance was made, the portal which combines these two extremities thereby sums up the whole sanctuary. It may be objected, as regards the cathedral, that the main motive for entering it lies rather in the altar than in the niche; but this in no way diminishes the significance of the West portal's niche-like form, which anticipates the apse, often called 'the Holy of Holies', at the East end of the nave; and the apse, which has the form of a large and deeply-recessed niche, serves as setting for the higher altar, whereas the main altar stands normally at its entrance. The message of the Christian door is thus not basically different from that of its Islamic counterpart; and each offers us, crystallised in stone, the harmonious complementarity between the first and fourth stations, that is, between cold detachment from the world and warm at-tachment to God.

Likewise anticipated in the portal, by the piers and arch of the niche, are the pillars and the dome, or instead of the dome the arched roof which replaces it as a symbol of Heaven in most of the cathedrals of Western Christendom. The second and third stations are thus also already prefig-ured at the entrance; and as we have seen, the first four stations, due to the Divine aspect in each, open out onto the fifth and sixth stations. These modes of knowledge

however are represented in the Christian and Islamic portals not by implication alone but also directly. It is on the
West front of the cathedral that the art of the iconographer
has had one of its great flowerings. In many cases it could
be said that the whole religion is there; and all is centred
upon the figure of Christ in Glory above the portal. The
majesty of this icon recalls the saying of Jesus to St
Catherine of Siena: 'Thou art she who is not; I am He who
is', which is a formulation of the fifth station, 'to know
only That which is'.[34] Moreover in many of the great cathedrals the West front taken as a whole conveys an impression of verticality and transcendence such as no visual
art has ever surpassed. But to return to the central figure
towards which everything ends, and which marks the final
reintegration of the temporal into the Eternal, its ultimacy
evokes also the subjective mode of knowledge, 'to be only
that which knows, the Self'.[35] For reintegration in its fullest sense means deification, which is the sixth station, 'to
become That which we are'.[36] In this same connection, as
a complement to the extreme transcendence of the West
front, the setting of the door in the niche symbolizes im-
manence, the Divine Presence in the innermost depth of
man's being. 'In all sacred architecture the niche is a form
of the "Holy of Holies", the place of the epiphany of God,
whether that epiphany be represented by an image in the
niche or by an abstract symbol, or not suggested by any
sign other than the purely architectural form'.[37] Relevant
also is what Titus Burckhadt says elsewhere, in connection with 'the niche-like apse' at the East end of the nave
of the early Romanesque churches whereby the whole
building takes on the aspect of a cave: 'According to a
tradition well-known in the Christian East as well as in the
Western Middle Ages, Christ was born in a cave, and this
cave was understood both as a metaphor for this world of

114

darkness and as an image of the Heart. This indeed is the meaning of every sacred cave: it is the universe turned inward, the secret world of the Heart... which is illumined by the Divine Sun of the Spirit'.[38] The niche is 'the reduced image of the cave',[39] and there has already been mention of its correspondence to the fourth station that of the microcosmic 'universe turned inward'. But like the cave, it stands also and beyond all for the sixth station which, as the abode of the Self, is 'the secret world of the Heart'. The prayer-niche must therefore be added, in this its deepest aspect, to what was previously mentioned, with regard to the mosque, as a symbol of the true Subject.

There can be no question, in Islam, of representing the Epiphany by any anthropomorphic image. But the prayer-niche is nonetheless 'illumined by the Divine Sun' through its association with the Qur'ān's Verse of Light: *God is the Light of the heavens and of the earth. His light is as a niche wherein is a lamp.*[40] *The lamp is in a glass; the glass is as it were a shining planet. It is kindled from a blessed tree, an olive neither of the East nor of the West. The oil thereof well nigh blazeth in splendour even though the fire have not touched it. Light upon light* (XXIV:35). Especially relevant to our context of inward depth are the different degrees of brightness which increases in proportion to its interiorization, first the niche, then the glass, then the oil, then the flame itself—the inwarder the brighter.

As to the iconographic splendours of the Christian sanctuary, their message is expressed in Islam, with no less eloquence, by calligraphy and arabesque. The two stations of knowledge are represented by inscriptions of verses from the Qur'ān, Divine Names and, less frequently, sayings of the Prophet. The modes of love and of awe find their expression respectively in the two contrasting kinds of arabesque, the rhythmic flow of stylised vinelike plants on the one hand, and strictly geometrical patterns formed by interlacing lines on the other. The two main styles of Arabic calligraphy may be said to lean towards these two modes of arabesque, which themselves reciprocate the bent: there is clearly an affinity between square Kufic lettering and the rigorous geometric medallions and other such ornaments, whereas the cursive scripts are akin to arabesque in the more 'musical' sense of the term. Much of what has already been said of the significance of the letter *alif* in connection with the pillar and the minaret may be applied to both the calligraphic styles: the great mosque calligraphers have always mastered the art of achieving a sublime effect of transcendence by means of *alif* and the other vertical letters, which seem to trace out the descent of the Revelation.

The revealed Word retains its exaltation in its descent. 'The Qur'ān is not created',[41] and therefore every quotation from it constitutes no less than a Divine Presence.

It must not be forgotten that one of the great purposes of Qur'ān calligraphy is to provide a visual sacrament. It is a wide-spread practice in Islam to gaze intently at Quranic inscriptions so as to extract a blessing from them, or in other words, so that through the windows of sight the soul may be penetrated by the Divine radiance of *the signs of God*, as the verses are called. Questions as to how far the object is legible and how far the subject is literate would be considered as irrelevant to the validity and to the efficacy of this sacrament.[42]

We have already seen the connection between the niche and the lamp; and now the context of holy writ, itself a projection of Divine Light, brings us to a more general consideration of the luminous aspects of the Christian and Islamic sanctuaries. In the former, wherever the windowing of the walls is extensive, light may even be said to take on an architectural function.

> The walls of Gothic cathedrals are not transpierced so that people can see out; they are intended as walls of light, or of luminous precious stones, like the walls of the Heavenly Jerusalem. Pictures as walls, and walls as light... The transparent pictures are like symbols of Holy Scripture, through which the Divine Light is made accessible to human vision; in itself, in its unattenuated brightness, it would blind the eyes.[43]

The Islamic use of stained glass windows is not to be compared with the Christian example just given. None the less the mosque also may have its 'walls of light', though this effect is produced not by transparency, but rather by its opposite. Sunlight tends to be strong throughout the Islamic world, and in various styles of architecture, from Morocco to India and beyond, sections of the walls are deliberately surfaced to catch the light and eject it, or in other words, to shine with a refracted splendour. One of the chief means of refraction in the upper parts of the walls in the *muqarnas*, sometimes translated by 'stalactite', which only conveys one aspect of this structural and ornamental device. The *muqarnas* is most often placed in the angles of the square or octagonal support of a dome, or in the vault of a portal-niche or prayer-niche. It consists of a number of small niche-like forms clustered together like the cells of a honeycomb. These elements are usually concave, but sometimes they are convex so that the indentation, an essential feature of the *muqarnas*, lies in the arrises between the rounded protrusions.

Light is always a symbol of knowledge, in objective or subjective mode, and due to its all-pervasive, penetrative and unifying power it symbolizes also That which is known, Transcendent Oneness and Immanent Identity. It is thus basically related to the fifth and sixth stations, and as such it may also serve to open one of the other stations to the vertical dimension.

> There is no more perfect symbol of the Divine Unity than light. For this reason the Muslim artist seeks to transform the very stuff he is fashioning into a vibration of light. It is to this end that he covers the interior surfaces of a mosque or a palace—and occasionally the outer ones—with mosaics in ceramic tiles. This lining is often confined to the lower part of the walls, as if to dispel their heaviness... The *muqarnas* also serves to trap light and diffuse it with the most subtle gradations.[44]

Light not only unifies the different parts of the building, but it also acts as a magnet to draw the soul of man into the unity which he beholds; and this brings us back to the worshipper as an integral part of the mosque or the cathedral; that is, its living centre. The purpose of all sacred art is to confront man with a symbolic representation of his own perfection which he is seeking to bring from virtuality to actuality; and the particular art that is our theme is all the more operatively effective in that it gives him a setting which he can physically enter and by which he can be surrounded. Thereby, in making him conscious of the dimensions of holiness which he carries in himself, it offers him its own various aspects as prolongations of those dimensions. From being merely an object outside him, it thus becomes, as his aura, one with the subject.

These considerations clearly apply, beyond Christianity and Islam, to all monuments of sacred art which are places of worship. To be within any such oratory is to wear a majestic robe of sanctity which is both a challenge and an injunction to the soul to make itself, by spiritual growth, adequate to this investiture, that is, adequate to the magnitude which was willed by Heaven for man at his creation.

## CHAPTER ELEVEN

# The Symbolism of the Sense of Taste

It is well known that Ghazālī on one occasion defined Sufism as *Dhawq* (taste); and in the third chapter of this book, with regard to the universal symbol best known to us by the name of the Seal of Solomon, we have seen that its two triangles express, amongst other things, the inverse analogy between the Spiritual domain and the psycho-corporeal domain of man made in the image of God. One of the results of this inversion is that the five senses, any one of which can be represented by the point of the lower triangle, have a direct perception of the Intellect, figured in the point of the upper triangle, whereas the mental faculties of reason, imagination, and memory, which rank above the senses in the psychic hierarchy, are altogether indirect in the way they work, unless they should happen to be, by an exceptional grace, inspired, that is, penetrated by the Spirit.

We have also seen, at the end of the first chapter of this book, that it is necessary to make a distinction between ordinary symbols and what we have termed 'sacramental symbols'. These, in their highest sense, may even be considered as identical with their Archetype, and it is this identity which guarantees their ritual efficacy, as we have seen from the last five words of the chapter in question, 'The Name is the Named'.

We will now quote from an as yet unpublished text of the late Frithjof Schuon in which he states the various needs which must be fulfilled in order that the rite may be effective. The text is entitled 'Pouring to Drink', and in it he sums up the central rite of Sufism which is the invocation of God's Name, in Arabic *Dhikr Allāh.*

> One cannot pour a drink when one has no drink
> (Name, *'Ism*).
> One cannot pour a drink when one has no cup
> (Heart, *Qalb*).
> One cannot pour a drink without making a movement (Invocation, *Dhikr*).
> One cannot pour a drink unless one's cup be empty
> (Poverty, *Faqr*).

*'Ism*: the Divine Element.
*Dhikr*: the Act that is human and Divine.
*Qalb*: the Place that is human and Divine.
*Faqr*: the human Emptiness.

There where the Name *('Ism)* is, there must be the Heart *(Qalb)*; for the Name requires a receptacle. Did it not require a receptacle, it would not be manifested in human language.

There where the Name is, there must be the Invocation *(Dhikr)*; for the Name wills to be assimilated and realized; God has revealed His name that man might live upon it.

There where the Heart is, there must be the Name; for the whole point of the Heart's existence is to contain God; to be a dwelling-place for the Divine Presence.

There where the heart is, there must be virtue *(Faqr)*; for the Heart must be pure that it be enabled to receive the Divine Presence offered it by the Name.

There where the invocation is, there must be Virtue; for the Invocation, being an act, requires an intention. Now, good intention is Virtue.

There where Virtue is, there must be the Invocation; for Virtue has its end in the Way towards God; its end does not lie in itself, any more then man's end lies in himself. The sufficient reason for Virtue is in the Divine Source, and the Invocation is the way that leads from the human to the Divine. Here and now; in the One and by the One.

This same quarternary, so eloquently expressed here by Schuon, is likewise contained in one of the most treasured and often recited verses of the Qur'ān, one that has moreover frequently throughout the centuries been chosen for calligraphic Mosque decoration. The words in question are spoken to Zakariah by the Blessed Virgin who was making a spiritual retreat during which he visited her from time to time in case she should be in need of something. The passage opens with the words: *Whenever Zakariah entered unto her in her sanctuary of worship he found that she had food. He said: 'O Mary, whence cometh this unto thee?' She said: 'It is from God.'* Then she added the words which contained the quarternary of our theme: *Verily God giveth sustenance unto whom He will beyond all reckoning.* (III:37; this same statement, without the emphatic first word, had already been revealed a little earlier, II: 212.)

*Verily God* is the name (*'Ism*, the Divine Element); *giveth sustenance* is the Invocation (*Dhikr*, the Act that is Divine and human); *unto whom He will* is Poverty (*Faqr*, the human emptiness); *beyond all reckoning* is the Heart (*Qalb*, the place which is human and Divine).

The first element in the quarternary requires no explanation; but for each of the three other elements there are questions which might be asked. As regards the second element Frithjof Schuon has said elsewhere that the Invocation is a Divine Mystery but that it is man who has to accomplish it. As to human emptiness he has said more than once that *Faqr* (Poverty) is the sum of all the virtues because it guarantees the total absence in the soul of individualistic coagulations which act as barriers between the Divine Qualities and the psychic substance of man. The virtues are nothing other then the imprints of these Qualities upon the soul. We must also remember in this connection the Holy Tradition: *Seek to approach Me by that which I have not*, namely poverty. In the physical world the irresistibility of the vacuum is symbolic of the attraction in question.

As to 'the place which is human and Divine', these words are fully confirmed by the following Holy Tradition: *My earth hath not room to contain Me and My heaven not room to contain Me, but the Heart of My believing slave hath room to contain Me.*

The Qur'ān gives us yet another quarternary which also corresponds exactly to these two fourfold earthly treasures that we have been considering, but which immeasurably transcend them, being itself not of this world but at the archetypal level, namely the Four Rivers of Paradise. To anyone who has read the seventh chapter of this book it will be immediately clear that the Rivers of Water, which are in fact mentioned first, correspond to that which is the primary essential. Without them the other Rivers would not be able to flow. As to what corresponds to the word 'sustenance' in the Blessed Virgin's answer to Zakariah's question, its Archetype lies in the Rivers of Honey which come nearest to being both food and drink. *God has revealed His Name that man might live upon it* is what the text we are commenting on says about the Invocation *(Dhikr)*. As to poverty the poorest person on earth is the new born babe for whom in the Divine economy of things, milk is providentially provided without any human intervention.

As to the place that is human and Divine which corresponds, in virtue of its Infinite capacity, to the words 'beyond all reckoning', the Qur'ān makes it clear that all the blessed Spirits are marvelously contented by what they are given in Paradise even though, as far as concerns the majority, they are also aware of the existence of more wonderful higher Paradises which as yet are beyond their reach. The most exalted of these belongs to the Messengers, to the Prophets, and to those of the Saints who are with them at the highest level of sanctity. They alone are mentioned as being given wine to drink (LVI:18–19), which suggests a certain correspondence between the drinking of wine and the infinite capacity of 'the Heart of My believing slave' which 'hath room to contain Me'.

The reader of Sufi texts as well as texts which spring up from other esoterisms must beware of mental rigidity. The word Heart, except when used of the physical heart, has always a transcendent sense, but it is used at different levels. In the hierarchy Heart-Created Spirit-Divine Essence it denotes, starting from this world, the beginning of transcendence. In the Holy Tradition we have just quoted it is clearly used in its Absolute sense, as also in the well known poem by Hallaj which begins:

I saw my Lord with the eye of the Heart;
I said; 'Who art Thou?' He answered; 'Thou'.

'It is the place which is human and Divine'. When the Qur'ān says: *It is not the eyesights which are blind but the hearts in the breasts which are blind*, the word can likewise be taken in its Absolute sense, but it can also be taken more relatively; and let us close this chapter by pointing out that what the Qur'ān says here about the sense of sight is exactly analogous to what could be said, in different terms, about the sense of taste.

It is not the tongue and the palate which are unable to taste; it is the dormancy of Hearts at the center of man's being which has deprived him of Taste *(Dhawq)*. This dormancy, which constitutes the fall of man, acts as a blockage in the stream of the Divine Manifestation of Itself. In primordial man that stream was not blocked.

Each of the five senses, namely hearing, touch, sight, taste, smell, is a direct mode of contact, in its own particular way, with what lies above it; and the essence of contact is identity. Hence the legitimacy of Ghazālī's definition of *Tasawwuf* (Sufism) as *Dhawq* (Taste). Hence also the legitimacy of terming the aim and end of the inner aspect of every religion as the Supreme Identity.

Ninth Century Kufic Qur'ān on vellum,
Chapter XXX, verses 25–27
From the Gulistan Palace Library
Tehran, Iran

The cover art is a detail taken from the above work.

# The Symbol of the Tree in Quranic Illumination

It is the function of sacred art in general to be a vehicle for the Divine Presence; and it follows from what has been said that the Islamic artist will conceive this function not as a 'capturing' of the Presence but rather as a 'liberation' of its mysterious Totality from the deceptive prison of appearances. Islam is particularly averse to any idea of circumscribing or localizing the Divine, or limiting it in any way. But Totality is Wholeness, and Wholeness means Perfection; and on the visual plane perfection cannot be reconciled with formlessness, which leaves us no alternative but contour and therefore limitation. What then is the answer? How can art conform to a Presence that is explicitly conceived as a union of Qualities, when on the plane of forms these Qualities are scarcely compatible?

The answer lies in the domain of what might be called the first sacred art of all, inasmuch as it was, for man, the first earthly vehicle of Divine Presence, namely nature itself; and it is, moreover, the Qur'ān which draws the artist's attention to this primordial 'solution'. There are few things that evoke more immediately the idea of perfection than a tree which has had time and space to achieve fullness of growth; and in virtue of the outward and upward pointing of its branches, it is not a closed perfection but an open one. The Qur'ān uses this very symbol of itself; that is, of the 'good word', being itself the best of good words. *Hast thou not seen how God coineth a similitude? A good word is as a good tree, its root firm, its branches in heaven, giving its fruits at every due season by the leave of its Lord. And God coineth similitudes for men that they may remember* (XIV:24–25). These last words bring us straight to our theme, for the truth to be remembered here, with the help of the tree as a reminder, is precisely the non-finite nature of the Qur'ān. A Qur'ān recitation must not be thought of as limited to this world for it has repercussions up to the Heavens, where its 'fruits' await the believer. Otherwise expressed, the Qur'ān uses the symbol of the tree so that it may liberate itself from being subject, in the awareness or in the subconsciousness of the believer, to the illusion that it is just one book among many books. It may thus be said to point a way for the illuminator, telling him how to set free from the finite its Infinite Presence. We need not therefore be surprised that one of the most fundamental ornaments of Qur'ān illumination should be arboreal, namely the palmette, *shujayrah* or 'little tree', nor need we doubt that it is meant to stand for the good word. The *sūrah* heading consists of the title of the *sūrah*, the number of its verses, and the word *makkiyyah* or *madaniyyah* to show whether it was revealed in Mecca or Medina. Written in a script deliberately different from that of the Qur'ān itself, it is usually set in a wide rectangular panel, often richly framed with gold and other colours, and with an arabesque as background to the letters. This heading is prolonged into the outer margin by means of a palmette which points horizontally towards the paper's edge and which achieves for the eye the effect of a liberation of incalculable scope.

The above quoted verse of the tree is immediately concerned with man's final ends, with the celestial 'fruits' of the earthly action of reciting the holy book, which is considered here above all as a power of reintegration. This aspect of the *sūrah* palmette is often confirmed by an upward pointing marginal palmette which corresponds to the marginal 'tree of life' in the Qur'ān manuscripts of Andalusia and North West Africa. But the ascending movements of return cannot be considered independently of the original descent. The Quranic text is equally insistent upon both movements. In Arabic the word for revelation, *tanzil*, means literally 'a sending down'; and the reader is again and again reminded that what he is reading is no less than a Divine Message sent down directly to the Prophet.

There are three main aspects which the artist has an obligation to convey if his art is to be relevant: the Qur'ān as a descending power of revelation; the Qur'ān as a mysterious Presence of the Infinite in the finite; and the Qur'ān as a ascending power of reintegration. The tree as we experience it on earth is a symbol of the last two of these aspects; but there is one verse in which the tree may be said to point in the direction of descent. *If all the trees in the earth were pens, and if the sea eked out by seven seas more were ink, the Words of God could not be written out to the end* (XXXI:27). Here the tree plays a negative part; but to be chosen for mention in this context has its positive aspect. The verse tells us, generally speaking, that earthly things are as nothing compared with what they symbolize; but at the same time it implies inescapably that the tree, for the purpose of representing heavenly implements of transcription, is a supreme symbol. One of the chapters of the Qur'ān, *Sūrat al-Qalam* (LXVIII), is named after the Celestial Pen, which is also mentioned, in the very first verses (XCVI:1–5) revealed to the Prophet, as the instrument through which the Revelation was made.

The Prophet himself said, 'The first thing God created was the pen. He created the tablet and said to the pen, "Write!" And the pen replied, "What shall I write?" He said, "Write My knowledge of My creation till the day of resurrection". Then the pen traced what had been ordained'. There are thus three levels to be considered. The Qur'ān as men know it is an adapted form, reduced beyond all measure, of what is written on the Tablet, which itself only refers to creation and not to God's Self-Knowledge. It is to this highest level, that of the Divine Omniscience, that *the Words of God* refer in the above-quoted Quranic verse. It is none the less an essential point of doctrine that the Qur'ān as revealed to men, not to speak of the Tablet, contains mysteriously everything, being no less than the Uncreated Word of God. We will come back later to this apparent contradiction.

From the point of view of descent, it is this instrument that the *sūrah* palmette may be said to portray. Nor does this constitute a change of meaning inasmuch as the Pen, no less than its 'consort' the Guarded Tablet, is in the direct line of the descent of the Revelation and therefore virtually identical with it. It is simply a question of two directions, and the 'neutral' horizontality of the palmette allows for its application to both.

The verse of the tree speaks of *its branches in Heaven.* The palmette in the margin is as near to a direct illustration as this art will allow. In other words, it is a reminder that the reading or chanting of the Qur'ān is the virtual starting point for limitless vibration, a wave that ultimately breaks on the shore of Eternity; and it is above all that shore that is signified by the margin, towards which all the movement of the painting, in palmette, finial, crenellation and flow of arabesque is directed.

Another symbol which expresses both perfection and infinitude, and which is intimately, though not apparently, related to the 'tree', is the rayed sun. Again and again the Qur'ān refers to itself as light or as being radiant with light; and many periods of Qur'ān illumination can give us examples of marginal verse counts inscribed in circles whose circumferences are rayed or scalloped. The solar roundels, *shamsah* or 'little sun', is used also of stellar ornaments, occasionally replace the rosettes which divide the verses; and the rosettes themselves are often made luminous with gold. Sometimes the symbolism of light is directly combined with that of the tree, as when a solar roundel figures inside the *sūrah* palmette, or when the palmette itself is rounded or rayed, with its lobe replaced by an outward pointing finial. There are other variants of the same combination; and what has already been said about the two directions applies equally here, for the Revelation is not only a shining of light from the next world, but it also throws its light towards the next world by way of guidance; nor can this reversed reintegrating light be separated from the soul's spiritual aspiration, which is likewise figured by everything that points to the beyond.

Related in more ways than one to the tree are the arabesques with which the palmettes, the roundels, and other marginal ornaments are filled, and which often serve as a surrounding frame for the main part of the page. Being vineal rather that arboreal, the arabesque does not by its nature point out a way, though it can give a clear indication of tendency, and that is certainly one of its main functions in Qur'ān illumination. At the same time, in virtue of its elusiveness, it constitutes in itself a mysterious and supraformal presence. It is also, like a tree, a vital presence and, where it is a background for the script, it serves to heighten the effect of the letters as vehicles of the Living Word. Moreover, as a portrayal of rhythm, by its constant repetition of the same motives, in particular the small palmette, at regular intervals, it suggests rhythmic Qur'ān recitations, which take place, we are told, not only on earth but throughout all the degrees of the universe.

With gratitude to the Thesaurus Islamicus Foundation for their kind permission to reproduce this excerpt from *Splendours of Qur'ān Calligraphy and Illumination* by Martin Lings (2004).

# *Notes*

## CHAPTER ONE

1. Italics are used throughout for all quotations from Scripture and by extension for such utterances as this.

2. The capital letter is used to denote the distinction. Moreover since this centre reflects a whole hierarchy of centres which transcend it, the term heart is also sometimes used of the Spirit, and ultimately of the Supreme Centre, the Divine Self.

3. This symbolism of the web has been admirably expounded by Frithjof Schuon, *Treasures of Buddhism*, (Bloomington, 1993) pp. 34–5. See also his *Atmā-Māyā'* in *Studies in Comparative Religion*, Summer 1973.

4. No single symbol can possibly reflect all the aspects of its Archetype. While it figures the outward impetus set in motion by the creative act, the web has no downward dimension. In this respect it needs to be completed by the Biblical symbol of Jacob's ladder, or by the Sufi symbol of the Tree of the Universe which represents the different hierarchic levels by cedar-like layers of branches, one layer above the other.

5. To take examples from the world of mammals in addition to the lion, with whom other members of the cat family are to be included, we may mention, as being truly symbolic in their different ways, the elephant, the camel, the horse and the wolf. On the other hand, in contrast with these sacred animals, the hippopotamus, the giraffe and the hyena are uninspiring, by which we mean, to revert to our liminal quotation, that their 'praise' is too 'faint' to earn for them, as such, the title of symbol in the higher and more exclusive sense of the word, though as animals, that is, in their life and consciousness, they are symbolic, as also in their very existence.

6. It is thus an error to suppose that blessed souls have to wait in Paradise for their bodies to join them after the resurrection, since if a soul has accumulated in life enough celestial gravity for it to be drawn towards Paradise as soon as it is liberated from its body at death, it will be reunited, once it has risen beyond the domain of time, with its 'already' resurrected and transfigured body.

7. That is, for the first and last generations of Christians.

## CHAPTER TWO

---

1. We owe this indispensable term to Frithjof Schuon who, no doubt more than any writer of this century, has stressed the need for awareness of the distinction *in divinis* between the absolute and the relative, a distinction which has always been known to esoterism, whatever the tradition, but which exoteric theology has refrained from divulging, more or less with impunity until now, when the widespread overactivity of minds makes its disclosure the lesser of two evils.

2. The word is used here in its original sense of *ex-stare*, to stand out from (i.e. from an origin).

3. See *Studies in Comparative Religion*, Winter, 1973. For a brief analysis, see Martin Lings, *The Eleventh Hour*, (Cambridge, 1987) pp.85-8.

4. That is, if the Exodus be interpreted, beyond its literal sense, according to its esoteric or anagogical significance as an image of the spiritual path, of which the ultimate goal is symbolized by the Promised Land.

5. See, in this respect, Frithjof Schuon, *Survey of Metaphysics and Esoterism*, (Bloomington, Indiana, 1986) p. 197.

6. We are not considering here the words 'intellect' and 'intellectual', since these have already been in misuse since the so-called 'Enlightenment'. Modern psychology did not inaugurate this violation, though it can be blamed for failing to react against it.

denotes exhaustion both in the sense of faintness and of finality. This last word is however a key to the *guna's* positive aspects.

18. See Portal, *ibid.*, p. 99.

19. *Ibid.*, p. 98.

20. The three *gunas* have their summit in the *Trimūrti*.

21. So named because he reflects the Absolute Itself, also named *Brahmā* or *Para-Brahmā* (Supreme Brahmā), a name that is neuter in gender as distinct from the masculine *Apara-Brahmā* (non-supreme Brahmā) of the *Trimūrti*.

22. Vishnu is sometimes described as *pītavasas*, dressed in yellow (see Portal, p. 44, note 4) which is also the colour of Lakshmī, his Shaktī.

23. In view of his initially destructive aspect, the connection between Shiva and Ananda may seem at first surprising. But it must be remembered that his alchemy prefigures the supreme transformation—in Christian terms the Apocatastasis—when the Infinite brings all finite things to an end and reabsorbs them into Itself.

24. A glance from the third eye in the forehead of Shiva reduces an illusion to nothing.

25. In Arabic *makhāfah*, *maḥabbah*, *ma'rifah*.

26. *Karma-marga, bhakti-marga, jnāna-marga.*

27. We must bear in mind throughout that each colour is a vast synthesis of meaning.

28. See Portal, *ibid.*, pp. 41–2.

29. As Frithjof Schuon has remarked, the Christian identification of these promises with the miracle of Pentecost does not mean that they cannot refer also and above all to the Revelation of Islam, for sacred utterances can generally be taken in more ways than one, and 'if Muhammad is a true Prophet, the passages referring to the Paraclete must inevitably concern him—not exclusively but eminently—for it is inconceivable that Christ, when speaking of the future, should have passed over in silence a manifestation of such magnitude.' (*The Transcendent Unity of Religions*, London, 1984, p. 116).

30. For the reasons why green excels beyond measure the other compound colours, and also for many other profound considerations with regard to colour, see Frithjof Schuon, *Spiritual Perspectives and Human Facts*, (London, 1987) chapter 2.

31. p. 28, note II.

32. See *Letters of a Sufi Master* (London, 1970), p. 11, note 3.

33. *Jam' aḍ-ḍiddayn.*

## CHAPTER FIVE

1. See René Guénon, *The Great Triad*, chapter 17 (Cambridge, 1990).

2. *In the Tracks of Buddhism*, (London, 1989) p. 141.

3. *Ibid.*

4. *Ibid.*

5. *Understanding Islam*, (London, 1963) p. 88, note 3.

6. Published under the name of Muḥyiddīn ibn al-'Arabī, but generally considered to be by 'Abd ar-Razzāq al-Kāshānī.

7. *Islam and the Perennial Philosophy*, (London, 1976) chapter 12. 'The Two Paradises'.

8. *Ibid.*, p. 208.

9. The number four for the Paradises must not be taken in a limitative sense but simply as indicating certain main divisions in the hierarchy. The same may be said analogously, but from a somewhat different angle, of the number seven for the Heavens.

10. St Irenaeus, later followed by the whole Western church until the Reformation, condemned as heretical the notion that all saved souls will go directly Paradise at death.

11. *Muhammad: His Life based on the earliest sources*, (London, 1983) p. 341.

12. This word, *siddīqīn*, is usually translated 'saints' which, if used here, might wrongly suggest that 'the righteous' are not saints. The word 'sage' serves to do some justice to the ideas of

wisdom and of truth that are implicit in *siddīq* which denotes a saint of the highest rank.

13. See above, p. 52.

14. Night in its turn has a secondary meaning of ignorance which veils the Divine Truth.

15. See p. 40.

16. *A Sufi Saint of the Twentieth Century*, (London, 1971) p. 225.

17. *Islamic Spirituality, Foundations*, (London, 987), World Spirituality, vol. 19 p. 238, note 15.

## CHAPTER SIX

1. *Castes and Races*, (London, 1982) p. 61.

2. *From the Divine to the Human*, p. 97.

3. Revelation has a prior claim to be entitled 'the language of the Gods' because it is so actually rather than symbolically, being no less than an intrusion of the Hereafter into the herebelow (see pp. 11–12). Even its verbal substance, in a language that is current among men in some post-primordial age, is incalculably and inextricably penetrated by the transcendence of its content. That language however in itself must be ranked lower than primordial speech, but it acquires the status of a 'sacred language' as the Heaven-chosen vehicle of a Divine Message.

4. See page 2.

5. For example, there can be little doubt that Dante was destined to play a positive part in the final stages of the crystallisation of Italian from Latin (see Titus Burckhardt, *Mirror of the Intellect*, p. 82).

6. *Paradiso*, I:13–24.

7. *Ibid.*, XXII:112–117.

8. The cave has also a transcendent significance, but by way of inwardness and depth see René Guénon *Fundamental Symbols* (Cambridge: Quinta Essentia, 1995), chapters 32 to 36.

9. Of Heaven, needless to say, the symbol of symbols is the sky and all that we see upon its face.

10. *The Merchant of Venice*, V:I.

11. In the Nordic legend, Siegfried is said to have been able to understand 'the language of the birds' as soon as he had slain the dragon. René Guénon (*ibid.*, chapter 9) points out, in this connection, that the birds symbolize the Angels; nor should we forget, in view of our chapter heading, that the Archangels are none other than what Hinduism and its sister traditions of Western antiquity term 'the Gods'.

12. Ideally art implies a full access—witness the word *vates* which identifies the poet with the prophet. But inspiration is not to be circumscribed, nor can it be denied that an artist may literally excel himself in his art, for *the wind bloweth where it listeth* (John, III:8).

### CHAPTER SEVEN

1. Far from being a 'concrete' image arbitrarily chosen by man to illustrate some 'abstract' idea; a symbol is, as we have seen, the manifestation, in some lower mode, of the higher reality which it symbolizes and which stands in as close a relationship to it as root of tree to leaf. Thus water is Mercy; and it would be true to say that even without any understanding of symbolism and even without belief in the Transcendent, immersion in water has an inevitable effect upon the soul in addition to its purification of the body. In the absence of ritual intention, this effect may be altogether momentary and superficial; it is none the less visible on the face of almost any bather emerging from a lake or river or sea, however quickly it may be effaced by the resumption of 'ordinary life'.

2. See p. 44.

3. *Mishkāt al-Anwār*.

4. In Genesis also the pure primordial substance of the created universe is water. *The Spirit of God moved upon the face of the waters.*

5. So too in Genesis *He divided the waters.*

6. *And thou seest the earth barren, and when We send down upon it water it thrilleth and sprouteth... that is because... the Hour is coming beyond all doubt and because God raiseth those who are in the tombs (XXII:5).*

7. To speak of death as 'a giving up of the ghost' is thus altogether correct; and it is because life is a presence of the Spirit, and therefore altogether transcendent, that it defies any scientific analysis.

8. The great symbol of life is also most precarious over much of the earth's face, especially in those regions where the Quranic Revelation was first received.

9. Ice and waves are parallel as symbols, representing respectively the rigidity (or brittleness) and instability of this form-bound world.

10. The Arabic letter *mīm* stands for death (*mawt*), and has the numerical value of 40. But this letter and this number have also the sense of reconciliation and return to the Principle. It is said that Seth was able to return to the Earthly Paradise and that he remained there for 40 years: see René Guénon, *The Lord of the World* (Ellingstring, Yorkshire, 1983), chapter 5.

11. These are the few exceptional individuals who are independent of any particular religion but who represent religion in its highest aspect, being, without any effort on their part but by their very nature as it were, 'throw-backs' to the primordial state of man which it is the purpose of religion to regain.

12. The Qur'ān here as it were extracts from Moses one aspect only to correspond to the symbolism of the lower waters, passing over his more exalted aspects which are the theme of other passages.

13. See Martin Lings, *A Sufi Saint of the Twentieth Century*, p. 134, note 1.

14. This is an altogether universal principle of the highest practical significance. In Hinduism for example Shiva and Vishnu may be invoked as Absolute, though their hierarchic station is at the level of the higher of the two seas.

15. See the poem quoted above on p. 57 and also *A Sufi Saint of the Twentieth Century*, p. 114, note 2.

## CHAPTER EIGHT

1. It is also the *nearest* of the European languages to Sanskrit, not only because of its undegeneracy but also by reason of its 'orientality'. Lettish, the language of Latvia, is the only other surviving member of the Baltic group of languages to which Lithuanian belongs, but it is less archaic than Lithuanian.

2. See Ananda K. Coomaraswamy, *The Bugbear of Literacy* (rp. London, 1979), and Martin Lings, *Ancient Beliefs and Modern Superstitions*, (London, 1980) pp. 8–15.

3. Luc Benoist, *La Cuisine des Anges, une Esthétique de la Pensée*, p. 74.

4. This is an essentially "lunar" function, and it is in fact to the moon that the mass of the people corresponds astrologically, which is a clear indication also of the purely passive character of that mass, incapable as it is of initiative or of spontaneity.'

5. René Guénon, *Fundamental Symbols*, chapter 6.

6. That is between the two world wars, until 1940 when the Soviet army occupied Lithuania.

7. This now very rare book was published in Lithuania only a few weeks before the war. One or two complimentary copies reached Western Europe but except for these it seems unlikely that the rest of the edition has survived.

8. The Sanskrit equivalent, *Dēva-duktri*, may be mentioned to show how close on occasion, these two language can be.

9. In Sanskrit *Parjanya*, whom the Rig-Vēda mentions as having thunder for his attribute.

10. *Alchemy* (Shaftesbury, Dorset, 1986), Chapter 11.

11. In alchemy the 'chemical marriage' is sometimes also called 'the marriage of the sun and the moon', but in the Lithuanian perspective the sun is always transcendent.

12. As also for the Celts and others. See René Guénon, *The Lord of the World.*

13. We see here yet another connection between Perkūnas and Zeus who is not only the God of thunder but also the God of the oak. Moreover, most etymologists are agreed that *Perkūnas* and *Quercus* (Latin for oak) were originally one and the same Aryan word. Its wide differentiation according to its Lithuanian and Latin 'dialects' is analogous to that of the word for five, which became in Lithuanian *penki* and in Latin *quinque.*

14. See René Guénon, *The Symbolism of the Cross*, (London, 1958) chapter 9, note 1.

15. A symbol, as we have seen, can never show every aspect of the higher reality that it symbolizes. To have a fuller representation of the relationship between heaven and earth we have therefore to conceive of the Tree of Life as a tree that grows not only upward, in the direction of man's spiritual aspirations, but also downward, because it is in fact rooted in the Spirit, that is, in the 'sun'. In the case of the 'normal' tree the sun is, as we shall see, the fruit; but there is no contradiction here, for the fruit contains the seed which is itself virtually the root.

16. According to Guénon 10 is the number of the circle, being the number of cyclic perfection. '1 corresponds to the centre and 9 to the circumference…it is because 9, and not 10, is the number of the circumference that it is normally measured in multiples of 9 (90 degrees for the quadrant, and then 360 degrees for the whole circumference).' See *Fundamental Symbols*, chapter 16.

17. As regards the relationship between the square and the circle, see Titus Burckhardt, *Sacred Art in East and West* (London, 1986) p. 18, and as regards the roundness of nomadic and seminomadic sanctuaries, see *ibid.*, p. 22.

18. René Guénon, *The Symbolism of the Cross*, (London, 1958) p. 52.

19. *Ibid.*

20. A doubly solar symbol, in virtue of the solar animal as well as the solar metal.

21. René Guénon, *ibid.*, p.52.

22. Rue (Lithuanian *rūtā*, Greek *rutē*) is also called in English 'herb of grace' which suggests that its symbolism was originally the same here as there. But already by Shakespeare's time it had acquired a somewhat sorrowful significance (see for example the last lines of Act III in *Richard II*), no doubt because of frequent punning on it and the verb 'rue', which, etymologically, is quite unconnected with the name of the plant.

23. This is a somewhat free though adequate translation of *kloti*, which means literally 'cover'. The reference is no doubt to the bridal treasure which the mother would store up for her daughter and which would not be displayed, whereas the 'share' is the marriage portion which would be assessed by the father.

24. Since light is a symbol of knowledge, reflected light, of which moonlight is the outstanding example, is a symbol of indirect, analytical knowledge. In other words, moonlight is a 'mental' feature of the macrocosm just as the mind is a 'lunar' feature of the microcosm; and it is to be noticed how persistently in the Indo-European languages this profound yet not immediately obvious connection between man (characterized by mind) and moon (Lithuanian *menuo*) is stressed by the recurrence of the root *mn* in connection with things or actions specifically mental and therefore reflective or analytical, such as mind (Sanskrit *manas*, Lithuanian *manymas*, Latin *mens*) and memory (the lost *n* is found in *reminiscence*, Lithuanian *mintis*, Greek *mnēma*). Let us cut short this list of examples, which could be a long one, with the name Minerva, whose bird is the owl, nocturnal and lunar, as opposed to the hawk, which is, as we have seen, the bird of Apollo (see p. 31, note 2).

25. The lost *n* is found in such words as *incommensurable* which are closer to the Latin *mensura*.

26. *Vainikas*, 'garland', is also the ordinary word for 'crown'. The star is not named; but if she is Ausrine, the Morning Star, then it is at the very least a remarkable coincidence, as the translator once remarked to me, that according to the Jew-

ish tradition Lucifer was, before the fall of the angels, Hekathriel, that is, the Angel of the Crown.

## CHAPTER NINE

1. The Spirit, in Islamic doctrine, is the summit and synthesis of all creation, opening to the Uncreated and therefore possessing implicitly, if not explicitly, the Uncreated Aspect that is none other than the Third Person of the Christian Trinity. According to the Shaykh al-'Alawī, in his treatise on the symbolism of the letters of the alphabet, the letter *bā'*, which has the numerical value of two, is a symbol of the Spirit. See *A Sufi Saint of the Twentieth Century*, chapter 7.

2. This applies not only to three in itself, but also to its intensification three times three.

3. In Arabic the letter *wāw* and in Hebrew the letter *vāv* both have the numerical value of six, and each constitutes, in its respective language, the linguistic mediator, namely the word 'and'.

4. This reserve is perhaps necessary because the septenary in question appears to be arbitrarily incomplete, unless we take the specified sins to include implicitly others that are not explicitly mentioned but that are none the less closely related. Above all, it must be remembered that some of man's worst excesses are the result of an interplay between two or more of the seven. By way of example, acts of appalling cruelty may result from a combination of the sins of pride, envy and anger, the more so if this self-deifying triad be based on an avarice that has become so crystallized as to preclude all generosity.

5. Needless to say there are many degrees of anger that lie between the two extremes; more precisely, though anger is seldom holy, it is often just and therefore often not sinful. The sin implies an extremity of violence out of all proportion to its cause, a more or less total loss of self-control and therefore of centrality, momentary suspension of all higher consciousness, whereas

holy anger is as it were an overflow of higher consciousness, a flooding of the periphery by the centre.

6. Saying of the Prophet of Islam.

7. This recalls the Quranic promise to those who sincerely repent: *God will change their evils into goods, and God is All-Forgiving, All-Merciful* (XXV:70).

8. See above p. 55.

9. The doctrine of the *peccata capitalia* can be traced back as far as Serapion, who was bishop of Thmuis in the Nile delta in the middle of the fourth century. Having given the number of the deadly sins as eight, he enumerated only seven, and on being asked about the eighth, he said that it was the elementary condition of the soul under the influence of sin, the condition symbolized by the captivity of the Israelites in Egypt. Now this captivity was an intermediary state between two freedoms, and eight is in fact a symbol of the intermediate or the transitional, which may be negative, as in this particular case, but which can also be positive or merely neutral.

10. As regards what might from a certain point of view be called its negative sense, eight has a 'mortal' effect upon 'five' (man), for the number obtained by their multiplication is forty, which in many diverse traditions is the number of death. Moreover, in astrology, of the twelve houses that make up the full circle of the heavens, it is the eighth that signifies death; and in this connection we may remember that the eighth sign of the zodiac is Scorpio, whose hieroglyph, the letter *M* with a barbed final stroke, is doubly symbolic of death, by the reason of the sting in its tail and because the letter itself stands for *mors*. But death is not necessarily negative, and if it be considered as the transition from one state to another, the 'mortal' symbolism of eight may be included in the number's overall significance as a symbol of the intermediate, which is what we are considering here. See also, in this connection, Chap. 7, note 10.

11. *Fundamental Symbols*, chapter 44.

12. As, for example, when he succeeds in drawing Moses and Joshua away from the very brink of the Waters of Life (see

146

above, p. 75).

13. The Qur'ān here represents Satan as tempting Adam, not through Eve but directly, and in other passages he addresses them both together.

14. It is unrealistic to maintain that no single soul can be held responsible for what has taken place 'throughout the ages' and that its responsibility begins only at its birth into this world. According to the older religions, which could still afford to teach, with objective realism, certain secondary truths that the later religions have seen fit to veil—no doubt lest their more limited adherent be distracted from the essential—our world is merely one of an endless sequence of worlds, a peripheral chain of deaths and rebirths that is termed by Hinduism and Buddhism the *samsara*. All faiths agree that religion is the sole means of escape from the periphery to the centre; but the doctrine of the *samsara* expressly affirms that when an individual enters a world, the particular heredity and environment into which he is born in that world corresponds exactly to the total 'earning' of his previous states that is, to his *karma*. The later religions may be said to imply this by affirming that God is Just and that babies are not born innocent, whence the doctrine of original sin. In other words, even if Judaism, Christianity and Islam do not explicitly recognize previous states of existence, reality compels them none the less to consider everyone as if they had come into this world with an accumulation of guilt already incurred. (See also, in connection with the *samsara*, Martin Lings, *The Eleventh Hour*, pp. 26-30.)

15. Abū Bakr Sirāj ad-Dīn, *The Book of Certainty,* chapter 6 (Cambridge, 1991). See also *ibid*, chapter 5 herein.

16. The reference is to the methodic question that formed the basis of the teaching of Srī Ramana Maharshi.

17. See also Matthew XXI:42 and Luke XX:17. It is not expressed by these words in their highest sense, as quoted by Christ and commented by Saint Paul, but in a more relative sense, according to which they are akin to the parable of the prodigal son. Their original context in the Psalms (CXIII:22) is directly

though not exclusively suggestive of this more relative interpretation:

*The Lord hath chastened me sore: but He hath not given
me over to death.*

*Open to me the gates of righteousness: I will go unto
them, and I will praise the Lord...*

*I will praise Thee: for Thou hast heard me, and art
become my salvation.*

*The stone which the builders refused is become the
headstone of the corner.*

18. This 'justice' is exactly analogous to the symmetry of
the majority of the stones. On the other hand, the lack of symmetry for which the keystone was rejected, and which is by
ordinary standards a deformity, is seen to be an extension of
celestial supraformality once this stone has taken its rightful
place at the summit of its arch and in Masonic symbolism, as
we shall see, the arch is one of the basic symbols of Heaven.

19. Much of what is in this paragraph I have already found
it necessary to set down elsewhere, with reference to
Shakespeare. There can be no doubt that in his maturity he was
deeply preoccupied with what is being considered here, namely
the development of souls towards human perfection, which presupposes the redemption and the integration of all those parts
of the psychic substance which are out of place. In more than
one of his later plays we are shown the sudden awakening of
dormant elements in a soul hitherto unaware of their existence.
Two of the characters in question are Angelo in *Measure for
Measure* and Leontes in *The Winter's Tale*. See The *Secret of
Shakespeare* (Cambridge, 1996), p. 67.

20. See *Muhammad: His Life based on the earliest sources*,
p. 330.

21. The Prophet's definition of the Greater Holy War.

# Notes

## CHAPTER TEN

1. His debt to *Stations of Wisdom* and Schuon's other books is acknowledged.

2. See Frithjof Schuon, *Esoterism as Principle and as Way*, (London, 1981) the chapter entitled 'The Triple Nature of Man', pp. 93-100. For 'character' one might almost say 'soul'. The intelligence transcends the soul by way of height as does the will by way of depth, but these two transcendent faculties are plunged into the psychic substance at their lower and superficial extremities respectively.

3. *No god but God.* This is the basis of Islamic doctrine and the testification by which one enters Islam. The fortress may thus be in a sense identified with Islam. But esoterically, since *lā ilāha illa Llāh* has an aspect of synthesis wherein it is counted as a Divine Name, to enter the fortress means consecrating oneself to the perpetual invocation of that Name, or by extension the Supreme Name *Allāh*.

4. Frithjof Schuon, *Stations of Wisdom*, (London, 1961) p. 148.

5. *Ibid.*

6. *Ibid*, p. 149.

7. *Ibid.*

8. The *alif* stands for *Allah*, of which it is the initial letter.

9. Frithjof Schuon, *ibid.*

10. *Ibid.*

11. *Ibid.*

12. Frithjof Schuon, in an unpublished text.

13. Whence the term 'exaltation' to denote admission to the grade of 'Royal Arch'.

14. René Guénon, *Fundamental Symbols*, chapter 41, note 4.

15. Frithjof Schuon, *Stations of Wisdom*, p. 150.

16. Frithjof Schuon, *ibid*, p. 155.

17. 'Spiritual action is, on its own place, a participation in Omnipotence, in the Divine Liberty, in the Pure and Eternal Act.' *ibid*, p. 149.

18. *Ibid*, p.152

19. These two epithets are used to translate *al-Bayyin* which is one of those Names which constitute the Divine root of this particular station.

20. Frithjof Schuon, *ibid*, p. 152.

21. *Ibid*.

22. *Ibid*.

23. Another symbol of the station of beauty and peace is the rose-window.

24. This reservation has its point, as we shall see later.

25. It could be said that in the mosque the nave is replaced by the central supplication of the ritual prayer, *Guide us upon the straight path*.

26. Titus Burckhardt, *Sacred Art in East and West*, p. 108.

27. Ulya Vogt-Göknil, *Turkische Moscheen* (quoted by Burckhardt, *ibid*).

28. Frithjof Schuon, *ibid*, p. 155.

29. By the time of the late Romanesque churches this had become the norm in Western Christendom, but the earlier Latin basilicas were shaped more like the letter T, with the apse directly against the transept. See Titus Burckhardt, *Chartres and the Birth of the Cathedral,* (Ipswrich, 1995), chapter 2.

30. 'When the main altar, as is often the case, is situated at the intersection of the nave and the transept, it corresponds to the heart in the body of the Divine Man' (*ibid*. p. 22).

31. Frithjof Schuon, *ibid*, p. 155.

32. The reference here is to the Romanesque and early Gothic portal in particular.

33. Titus Burckhardt, *Sacred Art in East and West*, p. 77. A note is here added: 'Sometimes the architectural form of a sanctuary is reduced to that of the doorway alone; this is the case with the Japanese *torii*, which marks a sacred place'.

34. Frithjof Schuon, *ibid*, p. 153.

35. *Ibid.*

36. *Ibid.*

37. Titus Burckhardt, *ibid*, pp. 77–8.

38. *Chartres*, p. 25.

39. *Sacred Art in East and West*, p. 78.

40. The lamp in the niche is constantly figured in the decorative arts of Islam, and in particular it is a favourite pattern for prayer mats.

41. See pp. 9–10.

42. Martin Lings, *The Quranic Art of Calligraphy and Illumination*, (London, 1976) p. 16.

43. Titus Burckhardt, *Chartres,* p. 105.

44. Titus Burckhardt, *Art of Islam*, p. 77.

# Index

153

155

# Index